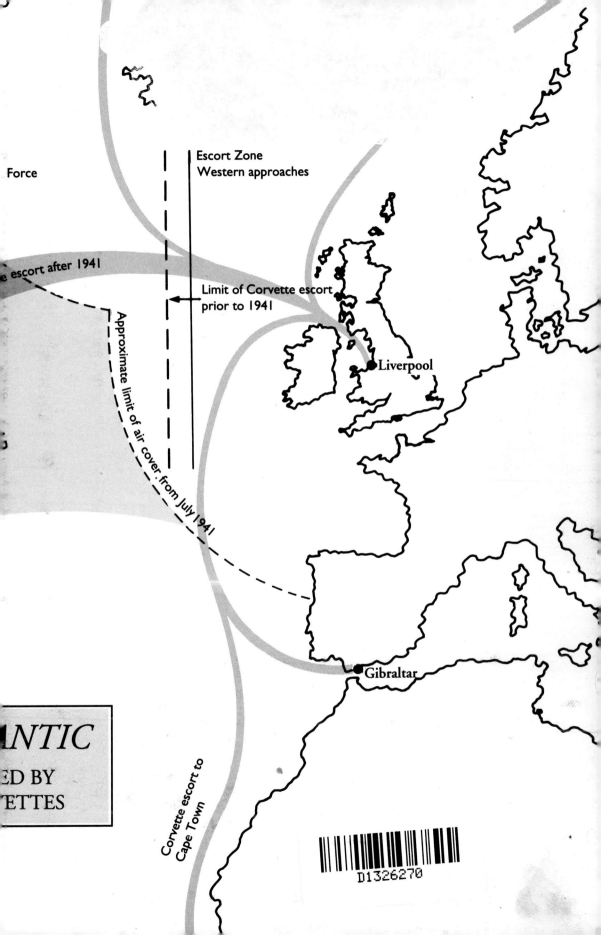

Force

Escort Zone
Western approaches

e escort after 1941

Limit of Corvette escort
prior to 1941

Approximate limit of air cover from July 1941

Liverpool

Gibraltar

Corvette escort to
Cape Town

NTIC

ED BY
ETTES

THE ROYAL NAVAL MUSEUM BOOK OF

THE BATTLE OF
THE ATLANTIC

The Corvettes and their Crews: An Oral History

To my parents
Bet and Terry Howard

THE ROYAL NAVAL MUSEUM BOOK OF

THE BATTLE OF THE ATLANTIC

The Corvettes and their Crews: An Oral History

C H R I S H O W A R D B A I L E Y

F O R E W O R D B Y C A M P B E L L M c M U R R A Y

ALAN SUTTON PUBLISHING LIMITED

NAVAL INSTITUTE PRESS
ANNAPOLIS, MARYLAND

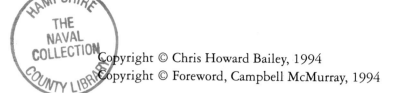

Copyright © Chris Howard Bailey, 1994
Copyright © Foreword, Campbell McMurray, 1994

First published in the United Kingdom in 1994
Alan Sutton Publishing Ltd · Phoenix Mill · Far Thrupp · Stroud
Gloucestershire
in association with The Royal Naval Museum

British Library Cataloguing in Publication Data. A catalogue record for this
book is available from the British Library.

ISBN 0–7509–0598–0

Published and distributed in the United States of America and Canada by the
Naval Institute Press, 118 Maryland Avenue, Annapolis, Maryland 21402-5035.
The Naval Institute Press edition is authorized for sale only in the United
States of America, its territories and possessions, and Canada.

Library of Congress Catalog Card Number (Applied for)

ISBN 1–55750–734–1

*Front and back endpapers: Convoy routes covered by the 'Flower' class corvettes in the
North Atlantic*

Typeset in 11/13.5 Garamond
Typesetting and origination by
Alan Sutton Publishing Limited.
Printed in Great Britain by
Butler & Tanner, Frome, Somerset.

CONTENTS

FOREWORD

'Oral history' is the term in general employment to describe the composing of history around the tape-recorded reminiscences of people who were either participants in or witnesses to the events or experiences which they recount. The expression suggests, perhaps a shade unfortunately, the introduction of a new and differentiated aspect of history when, in fact, 'it is clear to anyone who has taken oral evidence in the field over any length of time that compiling oral sources is an activity that points to the connectedness of all aspects of history and not to their division from each other'.

These words come from the pen of the late George Ewart Evans, for many the father of the subject in this country (*The Days That We Have Seen*, p. 4). Students inspired by his work have, over the last twenty years or so, turned oral history into one of the fastest growing methods of inquiry and data collection in the whole field of historical studies.

Partly perhaps because the small, portable tape recorder is a comparatively recent innovation – in practical form, it dates only from the later 1950s – there is a tendency to treat the results of interviews collected with its aid as being rather more of a novelty than they really are. In fact, of course, the current blossoming of interest in the techniques and findings of oral history in Britain and elsewhere is not the beginning of a new and original development but, rather, represents the first steps towards the revival, and reinstatement to its rightful place, of a once well-established and reputable branch of the historical undertaking.

The decline in the repute of oral testimony in the writing of history may be plotted in a rough kind of way against the rise of professional historical scholarship in the nineteenth century, the method falling into more or less disuse in the face of the overwhelming shift of emphasis in favour of documentary analysis and source criticism as the primary test of the historian's skill. The growth of history as a professional, academic discipline, and the systematic teaching of historical methodology based on the contents of the written sources, permitted the historians to retreat to the archive reading room and the library.

Segregated thus from the people at large, and free to pursue their own, microscopic concerns, historians became in large ways cut off from the lives of those around them and in the sorts of problems which engaged ordinary people – and, by extension, in precisely the kinds of questions which could have worked to promote the continuing indispensability of oral testimony. In any event, skill in handling and distilling oral sources ceased to be one of the distinguishing marks of the great historian.

Thus it was only in the years from roughly the 1960s onwards, that historians in the British Isles began to rediscover an interest in oral testimony. In North America, it had taken place much earlier – formally speaking in 1948, with the establishment of the Columbia University Oral History Programme – while the folklorists and dialect students, concerned to salvage the remnants of the language and customs of the prior culture, had never abandoned it. The widening influence of individuals like the aforementioned George Ewart Evans, whose published books had done much to hold up the possibilities of the tape-recorded interview as a legitimate historical source, and to reveal them to a wider audience, did much to rekindle interest in this ancient approach among social historians in our own day.

In sum, a development frequently looked upon as an upstart is nought but the continuation after a lapse of an old and well-tried branch of historical method, and treated – as all evidence must be, whatever its source – with proper caution, personal testimony has its place, and sometimes, where it will be almost our only source, its indispensable place in the historical enterprise.

***

Dr Chris Howard Bailey's work with the men who served in the 'Flower' class corvettes in the Battle of the Atlantic during the Second World War is a classic expression of the value of this approach. In broad terms, the history of the Battle of the Atlantic, the longest, most fierce and, on any objective estimate, the most crucial campaign of the entire war, has been moderately well-documented, certainly in operational terms, and to an extent from the viewpoint of both the victors and the vanquished (see especially, Stephen Howarth and Derek Law, eds. *The Battle of the Atlantic, 1939–1945: The Fiftieth Anniversary International Naval Conference*).

Quite a lot of writing in recent years has also focused on the experience of the merchant seaman at war, and over the period innumerable personal accounts have been provided, the work of participants engaged at every level in the campaign. On the other hand, comparatively few attempts have been made to examine in a systematic fashion the character of social life and relationships on board the small warship during the Battle of the Atlantic, or to consider the living and working conditions for the crews in such vessels, and the extent to which these circumstances influenced the effectiveness of those on board and their fighting abilities.

This book considers these particular issues. We have here a penetrating examination of the way in which the crews of corvettes coped with the exhausting nature of life on board, and the efforts they were called upon to make as a matter of routine to ensure that the primary objective of their calling – the safe and timely arrival of the convoy at its destination – was achieved.

The North Atlantic is bleak, blustery, cold, wet and rough, and for many who served at sea in those war years their memories are awash with appalling weather, open bridges, seasickness, unlit chart rooms and freezing seawater on the wrong side of inadequate, inefficient wet-weather rig. Escort duty in these circumstances was a miserable, exhausting business, particularly so in winter, and it seems likely that on any reasonable estimate of what could have been done to overcome the worst of these circumstances, British warships fell well short of what was desirable, and possible.

Thus, in corvettes, food was, in terms of both variety and nourishment, poor, while the arrangements for getting it from the galley to the mess initially hopeless; sleeping conditions were primitive; ventilation was inadequate, and it may be presumed contributed to the high levels of tuberculosis, and, certainly in the early years of the war, wet-weather gear was thoroughly useless. Little consideration appears even to have been given to efficient means of life-saving, either for the crews of escort vessels or for the merchant seamen. As the authority on the technical history of British naval construction, D.K. Brown has remarked in his article 'Atlantic Escorts, 1939–1945' (International Historical Conference to Commemorate the Battle of the Atlantic, 1939–1945, Merseyside National Maritime Museum, 26–8 May 1993, p. 16): 'with a little thought and some slight increase in cost, much of this unnecessary discomfort could have been avoided'.

In the exhibition at the Royal Naval Museum, which was the forerunner of this volume, some attention was given to these questions, but inevitably it was possible only to scratch the surface of the subject. Here, Chris Howard Bailey has been able to explore in a more expanded and extended way the issues which the exhibition addressed, and to do so in a way which allows the material largely to speak for itself.

At the Royal Naval Museum, oral history has now become thoroughly integrated in both exhibition and collecting strategies, and represents today the single most important component in our approach to twentieth-century collecting. It not only provides the most effective means by which to recover the past, but also yields a critical tool in the documenting of the contemporary social and occupational history of the Royal Navy.

It is my intention that this volume should be the forerunner of a continuing series devoted to the social history of the Royal Navy in the twentieth century, and beyond.

H. Campbell McMurray, Director
Royal Naval Museum, July 1994

ACKNOWLEDGEMENTS

This book could not have been produced without the help of many people, and, while I must claim responsibility for any errors, I nevertheless wish to thank all those who made this project possible. I would particularly like to thank all those interviewees and their families who allowed me to share aspects of their past and to present excerpts from their testimony here, and without whom this book could not have been written. I would especially like to give a very special thanks to: Dick Dykes and Geoff Drummond, who painstakingly read every chapter and offered insightful suggestions; the Flower Class Corvette Association, including Cyril Stephens and Mike Raymond; the Trustees of the Royal Naval Museum; H. Campbell McMurray, Director of the Royal Naval Museum, for his continual support, encouragement and learned comments; Colin White and the staff of the Royal Naval Museum for their help and support, particularly Val Billing for her general assistance and meticulous transcriptions, Janet Denby for her help with the processing of the tapes, and Assunta Del Priore for help with photographs; Sue Goodger for her assistance; Michael O'Callaghan for his designs; Reg Davis-Poynter for his care and insights; Kirsty Brindle for her support; my volunteers, Captain George Hayhoe, Carenza Hayhoe, Ken Flemming and Commander Tony Cowin; my doctoral students, especially Kit O'Connor, at the University of Portsmouth; all those who allowed me to reproduce their personal photographs here; Ian Allen, George Ambler, Steve Attwater, Pamela Bethell, David Enright, James Goss, Cyril Hatton, John Heron of Lumiere Pictures, Ted Kirby, Captain C.W. Leadbetter, RD, Edgar Pomeroy, Terry Rogers, and *Illustrated London News*; a special thank you must go to my family, particularly Cora, for their help and support.

HMS Azalea, December 1942 (courtesy James Goss)

THE INTERVIEWEES

JOHN ARTHUR

was born on 15 October 1920. He joined the Royal Navy in 1942 as a Commission Warrant (CW) candidate and was drafted to the 'Flower' class corvette HMS *Anemone*. He was later appointed to HMS *Duckworth* and was then given a pier-head jump to HMS *Newfoundland*, where he served largely in the Pacific. He then joined HMS *Swiftsure* and went ashore in Hong Kong as part of the landing force. Later he sailed to Australia on the *Swiftsure* and his last appointment in 1946 was as a lieutenant on the frigate HMS *Aire*. (Royal Naval Museum Oral History Collection Accession Number 4/93)

SIR ROBERT ATKINSON, DSC* *

was born on 7 March 1916. He joined the Merchant Navy in 1932, became a midshipman Royal Naval Reserve (RNR) and sailed the world on tramp ships. At the start of the war he was given command of HMS *Lorna*. In 1940 he was appointed to what was to be the first of four 'Flower' class corvettes, HMS *Rhododendron*, as her first lieutenant. He was then transferred to HMS *Azalea*, again as first lieutenant, for duty in Iceland. Then in 1941 he took command of HMS *Snowdrop*, and was on convoy duty in the Atlantic until July 1942, when he took command of HMS *Pink*, which was part of Vice-Admiral Sir Peter Gretton's B7 group. In 1944 he was appointed to HMS *Tintagel Castle*, then HMS *Tay* and later HMS *Loch Alvie*. He was demobilized as lieutenant-commander in 1946. (116/93)

DONALD F. CANHAM

was born on 21 April 1912. He joined the Royal Navy at the start of the war and was a leading seaman Radio Direction Finding (RDF) operator on the 'Flower' class corvette HMS *Alisma* from 1941 to 1943. (90/93)

HELEN CANHAM

was born in Southampton in 1916 and married Donald before the war. While Donald was away, Helen took over and ran his hairdressing business and can remember with pride her husband coming home in his uniform. She recalls also how important letters from her husband were to her and how she eagerly waited for the post to come. Helen survived the Blitz in Southampton and she and her husband, after the war, maintained their hairdressing business and ran it until Donald's death in 1993. (90/93)

HAROLD G. CHESTERMAN

was born on 28 February 1917 in Melbourne, Australia. He came to Britain to train and joined the RNR in 1933. In 1939 he was appointed to the Northern Patrol. In 1941 he joined the first of the three 'Flower' class corvettes he was to be involved with, HMS *Burdock*. He was then appointed to HMS *Zinnia* and was a survivor of that corvette when she was sunk on 23 August 1941, west of Portugal. After a month's survivor's leave, he was appointed to HMS *Snowflake* as lieutenant-commander. He was later

made her commanding officer and was in two major victory convoys, ONS5 and HX231. After he was demobilized he joined the Australian Commonwealth Lifeboat Service (Royal Australian Navy (RAN)) and retired as captain in 1972. (174/93)

RAYMOND J. DONKIN

was born on 28 December 1923. He joined the Home Guard at fifteen years of age. In 1942 he joined the Royal Navy and trained at HMS *Collingwood*. He became a leading signalman, was drafted to HMS *Wear*, a 'River' class frigate, and served on convoy duty in the North Atlantic for eighteen months. He was later involved in ferrying troops to North Africa and the Mediterranean. He was demobilized in 1946. (49/93)

GEOFFREY DRUMMOND

was born on 26 March 1922. He enlisted in the Royal Navy as a boy seaman and joined HMS *Ganges* in 1938. He became a leading seaman in 1941 and joined the 'Flower' class corvette HMS *Campion*. In 1944 he became a torpedo coxswain and joined another corvette, HMS *Snowflake*. He spent most of his time during the Battle of the Atlantic on the North–South Atlantic run and has been credited, as coxswain, with saving many survivors. Geoff retired from the Navy as a fleet Chief Petty Officer in 1973. (1/93)

IRIS DYKES

was born on 26 May 1921. During the war she worked in food distribution, serving rations and looking after troops. She also worked as an air-raid warden and did fire watch. She married 'Dick' on 24 November 1941 and after the war stayed at home to raise their two children, Maureen and Stephen. (435/92)

ROY F. 'DICK' DYKES, DSC, VRD

was born on 18 March 1920. He attended private school and later became a certified accountant. He joined the Royal Naval Volunteer Reserve (RNVR) in March 1938, was mobilized in July 1939 and commissioned HMS *Cardiff* at Devonport, where he served as a signalman. He was appointed a sub-lieutenant, RNVR, to the 'Flower' class corvette HMS *Honeysuckle* in December 1940. He became a lieutenant in 1942 and was then appointed to the 'Castle' class corvette, HMS *Tintagel Castle* in 1944, where he stayed until he was demobilized in 1946. He rejoined the RNR on demobilization and retired in 1975 as lieutenant-commander, RNR. He is currently chairman of the Flower Class Corvette Association. (2/93)

HOWARD O. GOLDSMITH

was born on 23 June 1922. He joined the Royal Navy in 1939 and went for nine weeks' training at Haslar Hospital to become a sick-berth attendant. In 1941 he joined the 'Flower' class corvette HMS *Snowflake* and remained on convoy duty for four years, eventually becoming a leading sick-berth attendant. In his last year he was sent to the Indian Ocean before he was demobilized in 1946. (43/93)

RICHARD K. GRANT

was born in Southsea on 19 September 1922. He entered the Royal Navy in 1938 as a boy seaman and in 1939 joined HMS *Hood*. He trained as a gunnery rate at Whale Island and in 1941 joined HMS *Polyanthus*. He remained on convoy duty in the Battle of the Atlantic until about 1943. He later trained on anti-aircraft guns at HMS *Excellent* and was eventually drafted to HMS *Armada* to join the Pacific Fleet, but the war ended at this time and so he was sent instead to Hong Kong and then Australia. He consequently became a chief petty officer gunnery instructor and remained in the Navy until he retired in 1967. (42/93)

WILLIAM HALLAM

was born on 5 July 1917. He joined the Royal Navy in 1935 and was with HMS *Resource* in the Mediterranean at the time of the Spanish Civil War. He was drafted to the 'Flower' class corvette HMS *Campanula* in 1941 and stayed with her for a year on convoy duty in the Atlantic. He was then drafted to HMS *Winchelsea* and remained on convoy duty in the Atlantic. After the war he stayed in the Navy, eventually becoming a petty officer stoker mechanic. He retired in 1962. (44/93)

EDITH OLGA HOLLINSHED

was born in South Wales. She met her husband in London and they married in 1939. When her husband was posted to Ipswich, she followed him and got a job in the area. She then moved to Liverpool when he was transferred there and they were together for three months before he left for convoy duty. Her memories then are of waiting for him to come home, longing for mail and rejoicing when he returned in his uniform bearing gifts from abroad. She remembers quite vividly that her husband was mentioned in despatches. (25/93)

MONTAGUE 'JOHN' HOLLINSHED

was born on 3 September 1913. He joined the RNVR in 1937, was mobilized in 1938 and continued training as a seaman. In 1939 he was posted to Harwich and then Grimsby, where he joined a trawler which had been converted to a minesweeper. He later trained as an officer and was posted to HMS *Heather* as watchkeeping officer. In 1942 he joined HMS *Oxlip* as first lieutenant and was on convoy duties in the Atlantic. He was also involved in 'Operation Torch', as well as the Russian and Mediterranean convoys. He was later appointed to HMS *Evenlode* and went to Malaysia, where he assisted prisoners of war from Japanese camps. He was demobilized in 1946 and was later recalled to active duty RNR in 1948, when he went to HMS *Northwood* and later commanded the Intelligence Department. He retired in 1965. (25/93)

RONALD JAMES

was born on 24 May 1919. He joined the Royal Navy in 1934 and his first commisssion was HMS *Iron Duke*. He spent time in the Mediterranean and was involved in bringing back refugees from the Spanish Civil War. He joined the 'Flower' class corvette HMS *Snapdragon* in 1940 as a leading seaman. He was mostly on South Atlantic convoy duties, especially those in the North African campaign. In December 1942 he survived the sinking of HMS *Snapdragon* off Benghazi. He was demobilized in 1947. (72/1993)

DENNIS JOLLY

was born on 10 December 1925. He joined the Royal Navy in 1943. He was a seaman on HMS *Wye*, a 'River' class frigate, and was then drafted to the 'Flower' class corvette HMS *Crocus*. He served in the North Atlantic and Mediterranean on convoy duty until he was drafted in 1945 to HMS *Ranee*, where he stayed until he was demobilized in 1946. (91/93)

FRANK G. RICHMOND

was born on 2 July 1921. He initially joined the RNVR but then was mobilized in 1939. He trained in gunnery and joined HMS *Circassia*. He was then on convoy duties to Canada. In 1941 he received his commission and trained in navigation. In 1942 he joined the 'Flower' class corvette HMS *Clematis* and was on convoy duties in the North Atlantic until 1944, when he was involved in the D-Day operations. After that he was on convoy duties to Gibraltar until he was demobilized as a lieutenant in 1946. (31/93)

CYRIL J. STEPHENS

was born on 3 October 1916. He joined the Royal Navy in 1940 as a Hostilities Only seaman. In 1940 he went to HMS *Raleigh* in Plymouth. He later joined the 'Flower' class corvette HMS *Orchis* in October 1940 and left in October 1943 as a Leading Seaman (Torpedoman). He went to HMS *Khedive*, to the South East Asian Command in Ceylon (now Sri Lanka) and he was there a year before he was demobilized as a petty officer in 1946. Cyril was the driving force behind the formation of the Flower Class Corvette Association, which he started creating in 1980 and of which he is now president. (3/93)

HILDA STEPHENS

was born on 18 May 1919. During the war she worked in Lloyds Bank in Cirencester and participated in air-raid patrols and fire watching for the bank. She also helped out with first aid when she could. She and Cyril married on 24 August 1942. Their marriage had to be postponed three times because of Cyril's convoy duties, but eventually they became husband and wife and went on to have four children, one boy and three girls. (3/93)

ROBERT D. TAYLOR

was born on 17 December 1925. He joined the Royal Navy when he was seventeen years old. He completed signal training and joined the Free French ship *Renoncule*, escorting convoys across the Atlantic. He was later involved in the Normandy landings. He stayed in the Navy after the war, eventually becoming a chief petty officer writer and retiring in 1981. (80/93)

SIDNEY T. WRIGHT

was born on 6 May 1918. In 1933 he went to the Royal Dockyard School and later worked on RDF at Eastney Fort East, where he was part of the team that developed centrimetric radar. After the war he stayed in electrical engineering until he retired in 1978. (92/93)

DISPLACEMENT 1,229 TONS
LENGTH APPROX. 190-200 FT.
CREW-6 OFFICERS AND 69 MEN.

An explanatory drawing of a corvette, as presented in the Illustrated London News,
20 November 1943, pp. 574–5 (courtesy the Illustrated London News Picture Library)

1. Depth-Charge Dischargers
2. Smoke Floats
3. No. 1 store
4. Engineers' Store
5. Petty Officers' Cabins
6. Depth-Charge Throwers
7. Carley Float
8. Engine Room
9. Depth-Charges (Stowed)
10. Vents
11. Bofors Gun
12. Shelter
13. Carley Float
14. After Boiler Room
15, 15A. Side Oil-Fuel Bunkers
16. Forward Boiler Room
17. Electricians' Store
18. Officers' Double Cabin
19. Dinghy
20. Galley Fuel
21. Crow's Nest
22. Port 22 mm Gun
23. Bridge
24. Navigator's Window
25. Direction-Finding Aerial
26. Wheel-House and Wireless Cabin
27. Ship's Bell
28. Loud Hailer
29. Searchlight
30. Signalling Light
31. Standard 20 mm Gun
32. Lamp Room
33. Dispensary
34. Officer's Single Cabin
35. Officer's Single Cabin
36. Oil-Fuel Bunker
37. Fresh-Water Tanks
38. Crew's Accommodation
39. Crew's Mess Deck
40. Quick-Firing
41. Windlass
42. Crew's Accommodation
43. Gas-Mask Locker
44. Crew's Accommodation
45. Fresh-Water Tank

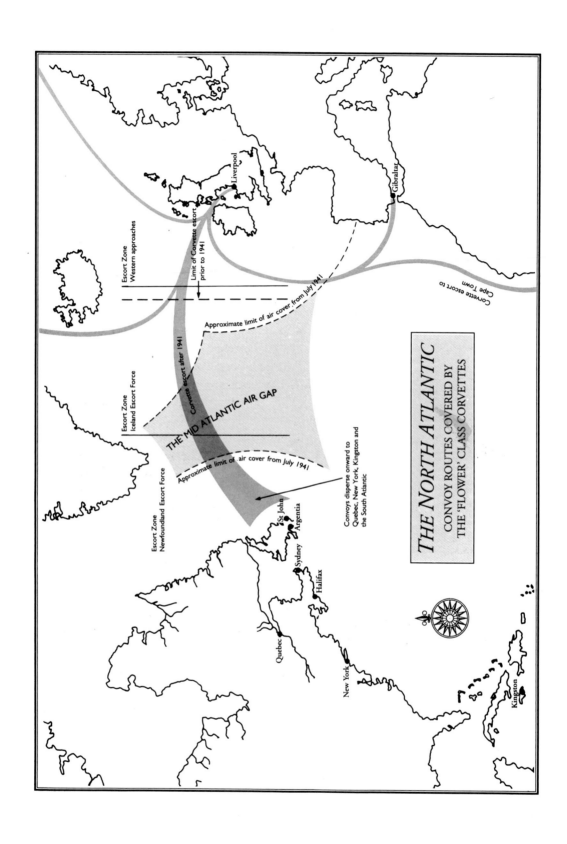

THE NORTH ATLANTIC
CONVOY ROUTES COVERED BY
THE 'FLOWER' CLASS CORVETTES

Escort Zone
Western approaches

Limit of Corvette escort
prior to 1941

Approximate limit of air cover from July 1941

Escort Zone
Iceland Escort Force

Corvette escort after 1941

THE MID ATLANTIC AIR GAP

Approximate limit of air cover from July 1941

Escort Zone
Newfoundland Escort Force

Corvette escort to
Cape Town

Convoys disperse onward to
Quebec, New York, Kingston and
the South Atlantic

Liverpool

Gibraltar

St John
Argentia
Sydney
Halifax

Quebec

New York

Kingston

INTRODUCTION

This is a book about the men who served in the 'Flower' class corvettes during the Battle of the Atlantic. It is based on a series of twenty oral history interviews conducted over a period of a year. As such, it allows the interviewees to speak as a personal and collective voice. It does so through the presentation in narrative form of extracts from the testimony of their experiences. Consequently, it is their story, told by them about the part they played in the Battle of the Atlantic, the lives they lived, the conditions they served under and the effects of the experience on them and their families.

The ships the interviewees served in, which have been immortalized in Nicholas Monsarrat's *The Cruel Sea*, the 'Flower' class corvettes, were small escort ships. They were built in a hurry in response to the Admiralty's decision after the Munich Crisis of 1938 to expand the Royal Navy in order to meet the certain threat of war with Germany. One hundred and fifty-one 'Flower' class corvettes were built in Britain and a further 107 were built in Canada.

The first such corvette, HMS *Gladiolus*, was launched on 24 January 1940. Their original design was based on that of a whalecatcher and they were armed with one 4-inch breach loading gun, one 12-pounder pom-pom, two Twin Lewis guns and two depth-throwers. Their displacement was 940 tons, their endurance was 4,000 miles at 12 knots and their maximum speed was 16 knots. They had a complement at this stage of forty-seven officers and ratings and their accommodation was cramped and basic.

The anticipated initial role of these small vessels was to escort coastal convoys, but increasingly they were used to escort convoys back and forth across the Atlantic. Their work on these transatlantic convoys eventually expanded and they became the backbone of the convoy escorts. Consequently, it gradually became necessary to modify them to meet the changing conditions of their work (their constant rolling, for example, caused major problems with seasickness for the crews), to introduce new technology, such as Type 271 radar, and to increase their complement.

All of this was accomplished while the 'Battle of the Atlantic', as Churchill had termed it, raged. This was truly the battle for Britain, as German U-boats and surface escorts struggled over miles and miles of wasteless ocean to assert their control over the movement of shipping. As Corelli Barnett has noted in his splendid history of the Royal Navy in the Second World War

(*Engage the Enemy More Closely*, p. 252), this battle, or perhaps more accurately series of battles, was fought between 1939 and 1945 on tactical, strategic and technological terms, all of which were closely intertwined and reacted one upon the other. By the end of the war, 175 allied warships and 2,452 merchant ships were sunk. Over 100,000 people died.

The corvettes and their crews were intimately involved, therefore, in the scenario of this complicated struggle: the allies to transport troops and essential supplies to a beleagured Europe; the Germans to prevent them from doing so. These crews were a disparate collection of men, most of whom were Hostilities Only (HO) recruits, many were reservists and a few were regular Navy. Most had no sense at the time of the large drama they were part of. Nevertheless, they came to be unified as a fighting team in a short time under extremely harsh conditions. How and why this was possible is a theme of this book, but the perceptions they have of themselves now are of a group of men who comprised an independent navy to some extent, with their own codes and sense of self. There is some hint from their testimony that they may not have been regarded in the same light as their colleagues on larger ships. Yet these men are rightly proud of the job they did, the sacrifices they made and the acts of sustained courage they all were party to and to which this book is a testimony. It is through this oral history, therefore, that we are able to get at an essential 'truth' of the experience of the crews of the 'Flower' class corvettes, one that, perhaps, has not been revealed in such a way before.

The research for this book was originally conducted as part of a project to develop an exhibition in 1993 at the Royal Naval Museum, commemorating the Battle of the Atlantic. I, along with team members from the Curatorial Department, worked with a committee from the Flower Class Corvette Association: Cyril Stephens, its president, Roy 'Dick' Dykes, its chairman, Mike Raymond, its secretary, and Geoff Drummond. All except Mike Raymond had served in corvettes in the Battle of the Atlantic.

The corvetteers put an announcement in their association newsletter of our upcoming project, requesting people to complete a questionnaire signifying their willingness to be interviewed and asking for any documents or artefacts they might be willing to donate to the museum or loan for our exhibition. The corvette committee acted as initial liaison, collecting replies, sifting and sorting material and acting as a contact for the respondents. From the replies, I selected a cross-section of possible interviewees based on the jobs they did, their rank, their period of service and the ships they served in.

In order, though, to balance the inquiry in terms of those who belonged to the Flower Class Corvette Association and those who did not, I found, through contacts we had at the museum, a number of interviewees, seven in all, including wives, who did not belong to the association. All interviews were indexed, had synopses completed and were either transcribed fully or extracted, and their extracts transcribed. Their relevant Royal Naval Museum Oral History Collection accession numbers are included in the interviewee list.

I have kept to as strict a presentation of verbatim transcripts as possible. I have also tried to keep the editorial comments to a minimum in order to maintain the flow of the narrative. However, if I have had, for the sake of clarity or by way of explanation, to alter or add anything to the text, I have included these alterations or addenda in square brackets. The photographs, with few exceptions and unless otherwise stated, are from the Royal Naval Museum's Photographic Collection. Many of these have been donated to the Collection by the interviewees or other corvetteers themselves.

In terms of the testimony, it is in the nature of oral history that discussions of its character as a means of historical inquiry often involve questions of methodology. Perhaps, therefore, some comments on this are not out of place here. Central to the oral history process is the interview. I have to go into the field, often to the homes of selected informants, and in the space of usually no more than two hours (although some interviews carry on over a period of months), encourage them to make public experiences that have often remained private memories for some time. Empathy on some level has to take place in order for me to enable them to tell their story in a substantial way: to get beyond the anecdotes they might expect I will want to hear. Most are not tutored in telling their stories and often have to be convinced that, indeed, theirs is a story worth telling, especially to someone from 'the museum'.

Once they are convinced, then I have to help them articulate memories that they may or may not have sifted and sorted into a coherent narrative. I must be as unobtrusive as possible, but nevertheless lead them. They are telling their stories from memory through language and silence. Some will tell them in a fluid way, others have to be encouraged with relevant questions, nods and affirmations. Often we go on a circumlocutory journey. They have a dialogue in their heads which I have to draw out of them. I, too, have a dialogue in my head: the topics I wish to cover. Yet neither of us can foresee exactly where the interview will lead. Often for the narrator the actual telling of their story is a sort of discovery. They are never completely certain what they will articulate as being important to them in the context of my questions.

In many ways, what my questioning does is to place the interviewee as the central character in his own drama. He becomes the subject of his narrations, a witness to his own self-dramatizations. Many express some surprise at this. They themselves have given their biography some articulated meaning which they have never shaped before. In the context of a life review this usually appears, especially if they are recounting some traumatic event, to have some therapeutic benefits for them.

What emerges, then, is a narrative on tape that is separate from both of us, but really something we have both created. The interview is a two-way process. Narrators only talk in relation to the questions asked, although they might fluctuate between expansiveness and reticence, and there is often much that is left unsaid. Yet enough is said to emerge as a statement of their perspective on the truth of their recollections.

Once the interview is complete, I then have a narrative from them. By narrative, I do not simply mean the written transcript, but the actual tape-recorded recollections which are oral and are composed of language, including silences, pauses, laughter and tears. All comprise the narrative. Together we have created a text. A text that will remain a statement of historical recollections, an interpretation of the past, for future listeners. My job then is to interpret this text in order to get aspects of its content back out to the reader. To re-present their history. In order to do this the narrative has to be studied. It can be studied for its structure, its textuality – that is, what it is saying within the text itself – and its social, cultural and historical contexts. Together these components give it some meaning as I perceive the meaning.

How the story is told is just as important as the story itself. Often I am asking the narrator to record what happened. There is a chronological sequence I wish to learn. But the narrator will often recall in fits and starts, moving back and forward in time between incidents along a supposed linear line. This is especially so when recalling a battle. Incidents flash into their minds, but not in strict temporal order. The narrator often relives the moment as he articulates his own drama. What I look for then is what appeared important in the telling; how the event took shape for them; why they might have chosen to recall one part of the operation rather than another; how, therefore, that incident appeared to take on meaning for them. The narrators are articulating how their experiences have made sense to them and how their lives have been informed and shaped by their experiences. Consequently, in such a context, not only the structure of the narrative but the actual words, images and metaphors chosen are important in suggesting meaning. Likewise, the social, cultural and historical referents contained within the text and the circumstances of its creation are important; indeed, they often reveal multiple levels of meaning.

The actual individual analysis of the narratives, then, is important, but, in order to get the material back out to the reader, I often have to look at a group of interviews to make sense of their collective narratives, not to get at what I view as the essential and singular truth of their experiences, but rather to see the collective sense of truth that they themselves appear to perceive. Obviously, there is an orchestration that takes place on my part. I am placing their narratives in relation to other narratives in relation to larger contexts;

namely, other secondary and primary source material. Yet I look for the threads that are common to the narratives. I see the patterns in their collective stories. I recognize that each story is unique, but I acknowledge that, to present that collective story back to them, I have to find some common thread: an amalgam of perspectives.

In doing that I must connect with them in some fundamental way. To a certain extent I must identify with them on some imaginative level. While my retelling must by definition be my perspective, I nevertheless strive to make it as close to the perspectives they themselves express.

Gradually, I build up a store of knowledge, based not only on the information contained in the narratives but on the sense of meaning the narrators seem to give to their lives. This is what we have in this book. The men of the 'Flower' class corvettes and their families have spoken about their experiences to me and in so doing have given shape and meaning to aspects of their shared past. I have had to find a narrative structure that best represents those meanings they seem to have conveyed to me in order to re-present them to a wider public.

Perhaps no one can understand the sea like a sailor or what it is like to have lived on board a corvette during the Battle of the Atlantic, unless one has lived on board a corvette during the Battle of the Atlantic. Yet I am dealing with people whose first-hand testimony is witness to that very experience. I then have to make an imaginative leap into their world and present their perspective on reality and capture their experience for public presentation. All I can hope is that I have done it here as they have trusted me to do it.

CHAPTER ONE

THE CORVETTES
AND THEIR CREWS

*When we went alongside the jetty
and I looked at it and saw HMS
Campanula, I thought, what is it,
like a glorified trawler.*

William Hallam, RN, 1935–1962;
Stoker Mechanic, HMS CAMPANULA

The crews of the 'Flower' class corvettes were mainly Hostilities Only ratings – they were specifically recruited for the war. A few were regular Navy, mostly young men not long out of boy training, and a number were reservists. Their training was similar: the boy seamen of the regular Navy had come up through such establishments as HMS *Ganges* where they had endured strict discipline. The hostilities only recruits had undergone basic training, not unlike that at *Ganges*, and the reservists, of course, who had long been familiar with the sea, also underwent intense training. These disparate groups of people had to be brought together as a cohesive unit capable of manning a ship and fighting together under arduous circumstances, and this had to be achieved in a very short time: the corvettes with their crews were desperately needed as convoy escorts.

'A Very Lively Little Boat'

THE ROLE OF THE CORVETTES

Up and down and around about. It pitches and rolls.
It's a very lively little boat.

ARTHUR

Sick yes. That was the first baptism of a corvette.

STEPHENS

Green seas over the fo'c's'le, so that one had to be quite
certain that all gear on deck was stowed adequately
and tied down.

HOLLINSHED

The corvettes early on were crude ships. They had a magnetic compass and that was the lot. The short fo'c's'le head. Designed by Smith's Dock at Middlesbrough, very much on the lines of a whaler, very good sea boats. But later they became more sophisticated, they extended the fo'c's'le head, they fitted radar, they fitted echo sounders, they fitted direction finders. They'd got lots of good equipment but they had a limited speed, that was the unfortunate thing. But they were good sea boats and by the time we got them out, we had none at the beginning of the war. I mean, we didn't get any of them out until early 1940, *Rhododendron* was one of the early ones. Then of course they built a lot of them, probably 150 to 200, altogether. Then they got the 'Castle' class corvettes, which is a more advanced bigger ship. And then they had the 'River' class frigates. Well, by the time these came into

HMS Clematis, *Freetown, 1940* (*courtesy Frank Richmond*)

operation, the work had largely been done. So I would say the 'Flower' class corvette was the backbone, that plus the 'River' class frigates, was the backbone of the North Atlantic. (*Atkinson*)

At the beginning of the war when the Admiralty needed many escort vessels very quickly, this [escort vessel] was designed and was modified to become the 'Flower' class corvette. And from the point of view of a sea boat it was excellent, even in the worst conditions that could be thrown at you in the Atlantic. But it had a lot of short-comings. There was a very short fo'c's'le which is where the crew's quarters were, hence the reason that in the Devonport refit the fo'c's'le was extended, but nevertheless, the mess-decks even then were always wet, because spray would come down the pipes in which the anchors and the chain were housed and so there was water everywhere. And in the wardroom flat and cabins there was always water, either from coming in on board, or from condensation, of course. I think they were around about 1,000 tons. I think they were somewhere about 220 feet long. As I said they were excellent sea boats. Very uncomfortable, I must say, rolled and rocked all the time and one had to use fiddles on the table all the FIDDLEYS time to hold plates and cups and things like that in place. Very small capacity for food storage, so fresh food disappeared after two or three days and for the rest of the trip across the Atlantic we would be existing mainly on corn dog, as we called it – that was corned beef, and hard tac biscuits and that kind of thing. (*Richmond*)

It was a pretty crude design. One could see if they had a short fo'c's'le, for example, how they were going to behave in weather. Very good little weather boats but terribly, terribly exposed, with an open bridge and a very short fo'c's'le. The crew going forward to the accommodation would be drenched continuously. Later they extended those fo'c's'les. (*Atkinson*)

We were asked [when they went as consultants to Smith's Dock] what was a corvette like. We said, 'Well, for the first six weeks you know you haven't a hope in hell of getting over that next wave, and then maybe, after the next six weeks, you think well maybe we will, and then after that you know nothing the Atlantic can throw at you will hurt you.' And he said, 'Mr Reed [at Smith's Dock] will be interested in that', and asked his secretary to ask Mr Reed to come in. A venerable gentleman, and Mr Edwards said, 'Will you repeat what you said about the corvettes.' We were puzzled, but we did and this Mr Reed said, 'You're being very kind to me.' And we looked a bit blankly at each other and he said, 'You know I designed them', which of course we didn't, and he told us the story then of how he had been asked by the Admiralty, I think probably 1939, to design a highly manoeuvrable, small antisubmarine vessel for the North Sea, five-day duration. And he was a very successful designer of ketches, and so he designed the 'Flower' class corvette for the North Sea, five-day duration. And then they had to go into the Atlantic because the Germans got down the French Atlantic ports as well and he told us that he protested strongly,

HMS Oxlip, *North Atlantic, 1943* (*courtesy John Hollinshed*)

and said, 'You can't send them in the Atlantic, they're far too short, you must put a minimum of 30 feet in them.' And the Admiralty apparently said, 'We can't, there's a lot of yards in Britain can build a ship 200 feet long, but no longer, and so I'm afraid they'll have to go in the Atlantic.' And so he looked quite surprised, when we told him how good they were. Uncomfortable and lively and wet, but safe. And it didn't matter what the weather was, we could go into the gale, across the gale, down the seas, and when merchant ships were heaved to with the wind on the port bow, or starboard bow, they could only run with it, but we could go anywhere. They were wonderful little ships. (*Chesterman*)

Well, it was like a corkscrew. About the third dip and you get tons and tons of water come over the fo'c's'le, and if you happened to be in the waist, you see, you probably get washed astern sort of style. But they had lifelines rigged when it did really get rough, but when we first commissioned, we were short. We had a little short fo'c's'le like a trawler, but some while later we got extended and it wasn't too bad then. But first go off it was rough. And the thing that was [annoying was] the noise of the cable going through the hawser pipes through the mess-decks into the cable locker, and all day long and all night long this chain was banging. And a funny thing when you got into harbour you couldn't sleep, because you missed the banging. (*Stephens*)

HMS Snowflake, *Atlantic, 1943* (*courtesy Cyril Hatton*)

The strange thing about *Anemone* when we first went out, and I knew I was going to be seasick, and I was seasick, and I felt it coming on, and I was always seasick for four days. And the way you get over that, you don't say, 'I'm terribly sorry, sir, I'm seasick.' You just got on with the job. You took great trouble not to throw up down the voice pipe or something, that wasn't popular. But I lived on hot water and Bovril and dry biscuits for four days and after that I felt marvellous. The motion of a corvette is something else. The description is really a cork on a pond when the wind's blowing. It bobs up and down a bit. But in heavy weather, the sea that's following you is higher than the mast of a corvette, so you're in a trough, and when you ride up on that it seems a very funny feeling like going up in a lift, and you get to the top, briefly look around and you see the other ships, and you go down again. So rough weather in a corvette is a fairly lonely experience I found. But it wasn't all rough weather, some of it was very nice. (*Arthur*)

They used to jump around. You could never guarantee like with some ships, you can say you're going to swing that way, or you're going to swing that way, but on them, you never knew which way you're going to go. Mind you, they were good hardy sea boats, there's no doubt about that. Good hardy sea boats. (*Hallam*)

A very violent motion. Particularly towards the end of a convoy trip. She carried initially 200 tons of fuel, but when the fuel began to reach low levels her motion became much more violent. (*Hollinshed*)

It was almost as though it was like a terrier shaking a bit of rag. You know the old ship'd wiggle somehow. It'd corkscrew up on top of a wave and you'd be up and you'd look down into this trough and you'd think, crikey, and the next thing you'd be down in there and a bloomin' great wave'd come over the top. It was a challenge somehow. You'd think, crikey, we'll stick this lot out and sometimes it was exhilarating at times, you know, you'd think, 'cor this is the life for me. It was alright when you weren't seasick, but when you were seasick it was a different matter. (*Stephens*)

Well, you were looking first of all for U-boats, to start with. Or if you were looking for a convoy or expecting to meet a convoy, that was before we had the RDF, you know, the Radar Direction Finder, you were up there because you were much higher up than those on the bridge, so you could see a ship long before they could. So you scoured the horizon to try and find ships or anything. But sometimes the officer of the watch would say, 'We expect to

HMS Oxlip, *1942; watch-keeping officers, bridge wing. Left to right: Lieutenant Coombs, electrical officer; First Lieutenant John Hollinshed; Lieutenant Adams, gunnery officer* (courtesy John Hollinshed)

meet a convoy at such and such a time, keep a watch out. See if you can spot it.' And somehow you'd see it and you'd report it and we'd alter course and pick him up that way. (*Stephens*)

[The corvette's] prime task, of course, was to detect submarines. But it had all sorts of other jobs lumped on to it. I mean, it got lumped into rescue work, [and if it was doing rescue work it couldn't do other work] and so I suppose from an operational point of view there must have been some really difficult moments for which I wasn't responsible. It was a general sort of 'Chase me, Charlie' for anything that turned up. I certainly think the merchant service found it of a great value, particularly as corvettes spent quite a considerable part of their time in picking up their survivors, which we were only too pleased to do. (*Drummond*)

Most of the time it was very boring, most of the time you were just waiting and watching and not ever letting up on your concentration, that was the hardest problem. You had binoculars, you were searching the horizon with those binoculars to look for periscopes, or to look for something, and you never let up. And you didn't because you know you had the pressure of knowing there was someone looking for you. (*Arthur*)

'Signed On As It Were'

RECRUITMENT, TRAINING AND WORKING UP

I went aboard Anemone *with my bag and hammock,*
that was your total worldly possessions and your bed,
and there was no particular welcome. We were just
signed on as it were, and appointed to one of the two
seaman's messes.

ARTHUR

Usually [at HMS *Ganges*] the training part of it started roughly speaking about six o'clock when you got up. The pipe was made, 'Hands to cocoa and wash', and you got some of the cocoa that bears no resemblance to the sort of stuff that you would buy in Sainsbury's today. It was slab cocoa, but it was very nutritious, and there was hard, sort of dog-type biscuits, which we all ate anyway because boys were always hungry. You then had some sort of work around the barracks or the training place as it was then. And then, roughly speaking, at half-past eight there was a sort of divisions. You then went on to various training, usually either seamanship, gunnery, some torpedoes, schooling, up until twelve o'clock when you went to dinner. And it was good wholesome food. In the afternoon every boy had to take part in some sort of sport – football, rugby, hockey, climbing the mast – all these sort of things, until four o'clock, which was teatime. You would have bread and jam for tea, cup of tea. But then you went to school between four-thirty and six o'clock – that was your school time. After school you would have your supper, which virtually was another dinner, quite a substantial meal, and then you had an hour's free time where you could write your letters, chat to your friends. That was entirely up to you what you did, and then it was bedtime. Of course, by that time you was ready for bed, nine o'clock, you know, it was really a full day. Quite a lot of activities, outside activities, went on. Sailing took up quite a part, usually that was in the afternoons. Boat pulling, boat work, all those sort of activities.

You couldn't smoke, and so smoking was quite a common offence. If you was caught smoking you invariably got what they call 'jankers', and if you were a persistent smoker you would get 'cuts', which would be six strokes of a fairly stout cane, not on your bare backside but over a duck suit, but nevertheless it was known to make your backside bleed from time to time. It was considered to be quite a severe sort of offence. To begin with you couldn't buy cigarettes. You couldn't obtain by ordinary methods smoking material so there were all sorts of devious ways of trying to smuggle cigarettes into the place and, for instance, if some boys who'd been successful at smoking managed to get some Players cigarettes in, you could sell one for sixpence, which was half a day's pay in those days. If you'd got smoking material you had no matches, and boys rigged up all sorts of devices. One of the more common types of obtaining a light was by arcing the fuse boxes with a bit of Bluebell, or a piece of paper dipped in Bluebell, and getting a light that way. Bluebell's the sort of metal polish that you use for cleaning all the bright work that they were very fond of in those days. So that in itself was just one of the bits and pieces that chaps got up to. (*Drummond*)

Petty Officer Geoff Drummond, HMS Campion, *1942* (*courtesy Geoff Drummond*)

It was mostly square-bashing and general drill. How to sling your hammock, all the general things that you had to know as a run of the mill matelot. And then after a fortnight of that you were more or less attuned. There was rather a funny thing that happened when I first joined. We were met at the station by a lorry, and we all piled into this lorry and we had no kit, we were all in civilian clothes. We arrived in the evening, I suppose about seven o'clock in the evening, we were taken to one of the dining halls and there was a table set out, table laid, very nicely, and a petty officer took us in and he sat at the head of the table and chatted, all very affable, and two sailors came in and served our meal, and we thought, golly, this is all right. This is good. And I remember the tea, it was tinned salmon and salad, and it was lovely. It was very nice. Bags of tea. And then the petty officer said, 'I want you to pass your civilian identity cards and your ration books round the table, clockwise direction down to me.' So we passed all these documents round and he collected them and counted them. And then his mood completely changed. He jumped to his feet, shouted at the top of his voice, 'Right you

Robert Taylor (arrowed), April 1943, HMS Royal Arthur

'orrible little men. Get on your feet.' It was just as though the whole thing completely changed. And we then doubled out and doubled off to our kitting out, to get our kit, and then off to our billets. And at the end of that fortnight, I think every single man of us regretted ever having heard of the Navy. But it was a good thing, because after that it was easy – after that first fortnight.

Training was very basic indeed. I mean, looking back on it, I didn't have very much chance to get any experience of actual medical work on wards that was going to be of any service. Looking back, I'd be horrified now if I had to do nine weeks training like that and then be bunged on a ship, as virtually ship's doctor. Because there was no doctor carried, I was the only medical rating on board looking after the health of eighty men. But you took it in your stride, you didn't think much of it at the time. But I'd find it a bit mind-boggling now. (*Goldsmith*)

I went back into the Navy. I joined up again, was called up and went through to HMS *Glendower*, which was a Butlin's holiday camp in Wales. From there I was at that stage selected as potential officer material. Went through a selection board and became what is known as a CW rating. CW ratings weren't paid any different. It was the question of a description rather than rank. CW rating, and we didn't ask what it meant. [A CW candidate was a wardroom candidate, but the initials of this were reversed to CW candidate as it would have been a big laugh if they were called WC candidates. A commission warrant was a different process. As far as I remember, very few

HOs, if any, would have had time to get selected for that. (Drummond)] Now from there I went to Chatham, the Royal Naval Barracks, Chatham, where it was quite an interesting eye-opener to the Navy, polishing the floors. I served in a diving boat, which meant you sat out in the middle of the Medway winding a pump round to give the air to the divers down below.

Strictness in the Navy was nothing like I'd expected. Chief gunner's mates were the ones to worry about because they were always wearing gaiters, and if you were walking when you should have been doubling, then you got a real balling out. But on the whole it was very much a sort of family. On the diving boat we all sat round in a mess, about eight of us, and one of us did the cooking – cook of the mess – at the end of the pier in a little hut. It was great. Some of the other things we did was to make cigarettes for the Chief Petty Officers, which I think was a little perk that they had. But Chatham was quite interesting. We slept in chalk tunnels at night because of air raids, and slung our hammocks on the steels that supported the things. There were no air raids when I was there. I was then called as a CW rating. You know you weren't trained as a CW, you were selected. You had a thing which I believe was called OLQ: 'Officer Like Qualities'. It was a bit of a joke. They needed officers and they had to find them from the ranks. There was no great merit. If you were a bit of a pusher, well, I was keen. And I suppose that was the penalty for keenness. They thought well we'll give him a short term and they wanted to put me onto a paddlesteamer working out from south pier, and I thought, I want to go to sea, and they said, 'Well you asked for it', and they called me back and drafted me to a corvette, HMS *Anemone*. (*Arthur*)

[I went] on to the dock, by which time it was light. And when we arrived, the tide was out and there was no sign of a ship, until we walked to the edge of the dock and looked down and there was this tiny little ship, [HMS *Snowflake*]. None of us could believe that that was what we were going to. It was rusty. It was covered in pipes and cables. There were dockyard mateys crawling all over it. And we all went aboard. There was no electricity. It was freezing cold, pitch black. We were finding our way round with torches. And I think every man Jack of us felt thoroughly miserable. But, however, it was eventually all tidied up, cleaned up and made ship-shape and Bristol fashion, and we did our sea trials and it very soon became obvious that it was a cracking little ship. (*Goldsmith*)

Then we went up to Tobermory, for working up trials. There was an old admiral [Commodore (Vice-Admiral retired) G.O. Stephenson, of HMS *Western Isles* in the Inner Hebrides, known as the 'Terror of Tobermory'] in charge, and at night he sent the commandoes aboard to our signal office and

HMS Snowflake, *North Atlantic, 1942* (*courtesy Geoff Drummond*)

go through our code books, and sent us a signal in code next day. It was pretty tough up there, and the only thing ashore was a brewery and nothing else, when [the crews] did get ashore. It was pretty bleak up there. (*Donkin*)

Tobermory, oh my God, it was murder. We had this Commodore Stephenson, 'Monkey Brand', they nicknamed him. He used to have two little tufts on his face. And he was about seventy odd, and [he and his training staff would] come aboard any time of the night, any time of night they'd come and board your ship and if he was a bosun's quartermaster, I mean he had to keep watch quarter-deck and fo'c's'le, and any boats approaching, because you stood out in harbour, you anchored out there or on to a buoy, and they'd come and board you in the middle of the night. So you had to keep a good watch. It was a building-up course. We dropped a clanger when we went in there. We hit another ship in the stern, HMS *Cam*, she'd come for a build-up course as well, and we gave her a little push at the back, and this commodore made 'em put new plates in the bows. Everybody thought they were going to Liverpool to get a bit of leave or something. He says, 'No, rig the stages, seamen rig the stages, ERAs [Engine Room Artificers] and people, do the repairs.' And he made them do it in the harbour.

It was him who used to sort us out in the working up trials and he had some quite funny tricks he used to do. He'd allocate a ship to raid another ship during the night and pinch anything they could find, like the log books or gun off the bridge or something like that, and woe betide the officer next morning. When we used to go out on trials we used to go out with a tracker

Tobermory, 1943 (courtesy Dennis Jolly)

submarine, and on the way back in you throw a lifebelt over the side. If you were seaboat's crew you'd have to row and get this blasted thing, but he was a very tough sort of a customer this Monkey Stephenson. You'd come on board and you'd have exercises: 'abandon ship', 'collision at sea', 'fire in the galley', 'fire somewhere else', pipes and wires all over the place, but in the finish we knuckled down. (*Stephens*)

When we first commissioned, towards the end of June in 1941, we had trials, we went up to Tobermory, and Tobermory was a bit like Portland, Flag Officer Sea Training. They had the 'Terror of Tobermory' up there. And everybody there at any time of the day or night could be called upon to do some particular task as a ship. And basically that's about all the training we got. We went straight from that training on to a convoy – OG71 – where we lost quite a number of ships. Now what that did to those sort of lads I don't really know. But one thing that is for sure, they soon became experienced. They really did become experienced. (*Drummond*)

That was a lovely place, Tobermory. Tobermory was a beautiful place. We did our trials with aircraft, our own aircraft, flying at night, submarine trials. And they had a mobile cinema used to come round, I remember that. And we used to go ashore and see [instructional films]. But the people were so lovely at Tobermory. (*James*)

Our first assignment, when we eventually got out of Belfast, [was to go] to Tobermory, and I shall never forget that, never forget that. I went into the wheelhouse and the wheelhouse door blew and it caught my finger, and what with that and being seasick I thought, well, this is the end.

We went down to Newport in Wales to have a new asdic dome fitted and we came back, did working up trials again and then we were allocated to B4 group. We were on B4 group for a while, and then eventually went on to B3. It was a different flotilla leader. They were doing exactly the same trip across the Atlantic but we were allocated to B3 in the finish. (*Stephens*)

'Painters, Bricklayers, Carpenters, Hairdressers'
THE STRUCTURE OF THE CREW

*I think once you've got some leading seamen with you
and active service ratings who know the drill, it's much
easier. I think they looked upon us at first as though we
were something like – well I don't know what they
thought of us, because you see there were painters,
bricklayers, carpenters, hairdressers, you know, to form
the ship's company on board a corvette.*

STEPHENS

In our particular ship, our captain was an RNVR. He was a two-and-a-half ring chap called Johnson. In fact we used to nickname him 'Star Shell' Johnson, that was his nickname. And he was a great guy, no two ways about that. We had an RNR officer as the first lieutenant, and the rest of them were all RNVRs. The three youngest sub-lieutenants were virtually straight from training. I think they had very little experience of what was going on. Most of the crew would be Hostilities Only, but there were a nucleus of what you would call RN ratings. They were chaps like myself who'd been in just before the war or who'd been recalled, having served before the war. But they would be the coxswain of the ship, the chief bosun's mate of the ship, the chief engineer, who would be an ERA [Engine Room Artificer] or a [chief] mechanician, two or three stoker petty officers, who were also engine room personnel, leading stoker, who would be RN, and one or two stokers. From the seamen point of view, I think I was one of three leading hands who was RN. We had two or three ex-fishermen, able seamen, who were really staunch chaps, you know. They'd been seamen all their lives. They were deep-sea seamen. I don't recall we had any ABs [Able Seaman] who were RN, but all the remainder were Hostilities Only. The leading signalman, he was RN, but

HMS Poppy, *Les Floyd, signalman, 'Blackie', Londonderry, 1943* (courtesy Ted Kirby)

the other two that was on there they were HO. Coders came into the Navy. They were HO, so basically [the crew] were a Hostilities Only crew, although you had a nucleus of RN ratings. I think that's how the Navy had worked it, you know, during the war. (*Drummond*)

They soon became experienced, they really did, yes they did. They were living the life all day long, every day. Didn't take you long to learn how to steer a ship. Again, if action stations was sounded the coxswain would take over the wheel, that sort of thing, you see. Down in the engine room and the boiler room, the engineer chief mechanic, he would be active service, or even a Royal Fleet Reservist that's called back. The Royal Fleet Reservists were active servicemen who'd retired or finished their time and then went on to the Royal Fleet Reserve, and they were called back into these positions of responsibility. And under them would be stokers, of all sorts, some with experience of engines, but basically they were Hostilities Only seamen, just the same seamen, some had never seen the sea before they joined our ship. (Dykes) Well, the skipper was generally RNR, and ours was Captain White, and then you had a first lieutenant who could have been RNR as well. And then you had sub-lieutenants RNVR. You'd have two leading seamen as part of the seaman's branch and you'd have a stoker PO and leading seaman in the stoker's branch and then you'd have a chief ERA, and then you'd have the coxswain who was responsible to the captain, and then you'd have the buffer who was responsible to the first lieutenant working part of the ship. We were allocated into watches – red, white and blue – with probably an AB in charge.

When we first commissioned we had one leading seaman who was an acid type, you know, he was a real acid type. Everything was per book. But we had one able seaman there, Tom Cox, who more or less stood up for us HOs because honestly we didn't know the front end of a ship from the back really. But after a few weeks we gradually began to knuckle down, you know, began to get the feel of the ship and what we were supposed to do, and in the end it built up a confidence between the active service ratings and the HOs. And the time came when, if you were a seaman, you were allocated to have a watch on the wheel, under the eyes of the quartermaster. The [QM] would shout up to the officer of the watch who was on the wheel that so and so was going to take over, and he'd stand by him to keep an eye on him. (*Stephens*)

When I joined *Campion* it was much more free and easy. And I was not exactly distrustful, but I sometimes thought you were being tested out by different things. The younger officers were quite inexperienced, I don't think they had had any experience really in what you might call handling people, but there was never any trouble. The skipper was good. He had had some experience with it. It was free and easy. I had a name for it: it was a bit of a Harry Tate's navy, you know. It was a bit come as you please. I think as long as you could do your job, everything went all right really.

The officers were just the same as anybody else looking for promotion. There were some times when they wanted to do it in the RN style, but of course they lacked the experience. When we say the RN style, there was a complete difference going from a peace time navy to a war time navy, and the things that you did in peace time you wouldn't necessarily want to do in war time, certainly not on board a small ship. Divisions, all dressing up in your best gear. If you were on a cruiser, you had to change into night clothing, which was a blue suit without a collar. Now, if subsequently you were called away for action stations or something like that, you went there in that particular rig. Whereas on the corvette, if you were called away to go into your lifeboat and then you had to pick up survivors [covered in oil], you were in the wrong rig, you see. We'd go in a pair of overalls or something like that. (*Drummond*)

The mess mates I had were a real mixture. There was a fisherman from the Outer Hebrides, whose name was MacCleod, a very dour fellow, but really helpful. There was a merchant seaman from Liverpool, who was Jock something or other, and he taught me a great deal about seamanship, as you can expect. We had one or two regular naval ratings on board. The gun-layer was a leading hand. The coxswain is a senior petty officer on board a corvette, and he was the one ultimately responsible for discipline. He'd combine the role of master-at-arms as well, and if anybody was in trouble, the coxswain brought him up before the first lieutenant, that sort of thing. But on the whole there was a great friendliness, and you were accepted. (*Arthur*)

I think people got on well. You had quite a mixture, you had a geographical mixture as well. I mean you might get people from Scotland or people from Wales or from Yorkshire. I think these men had a great camaraderie. You were expected to do anything. You always had a coxswain who was probably Royal Navy and accustomed to discipline and what should and shouldn't be done at times like 'up-spirits', for example. Discipline was important, but there was a rare case of a baddy. (*Atkinson*)

The discipline was largely self-imposed. It wasn't a question of rules. It was self-imposed because it was survival. People were not late on watch, people did keep a good look out and it didn't need anybody to tell them either. It was very much a self-imposed discipline, which I suppose was what was

HMS Snowflake, *a deck working party, Atlantic, 1943* (*courtesy Cyril Hatton*)

special about a corvette. There was very little imposed discipline. You saluted as a matter of course and you said, 'Aye, aye sir', and you repeated things back, because it was sensible to do so. There was very little occasion for marching up and down as it were. Big ships, yes, bigger ships you have a great deal more bullshit. But that was the way corvettes were: very special. It was a family and it ran itself. That was my feeling. (*Arthur*)

Ours was a happy ship, very happy ship. Because mainly from their point of view, the chaps that were called up, there was little or no discipline at all. When your watch came up you turned up on watch and when you weren't on watch that was it. And as I say, we didn't have Sunday divisions and marching around with rifles and having to wear our full uniform and that sort of thing. As a matter of fact, except for the conditions, the living conditions and lack of facilities, it was much better being on those ships than it was on the battleships or the cruisers.

We were a small, closely knit unit that only used discipline that was actually necessary. A lot depended on the captain. I had two good captains and you were all chums together and you all were doing the same sort of job and everyone looked after one another. All the time I was on board I never saw a fight – I've heard voices raised in anger, but I've never seen a fight on one of those ships. I've seen them on bigger ships, but not on [corvettes]. (*Grant*)

I think I found myself amongst a lot of friends. Not people who were obviously friendly, but people who acted friendly. You were accepted into the family quite quickly. There was a great division [though] between the wardroom and the lower deck which was not breached very much. Socially ashore, there was no contact, which strangely enough in the Navy the Americans didn't understand and the Australians certainly didn't, the fact that you were on the same ship but one was wardroom and one was mess-deck, it was very embarrassing for both. So the mess-deck kept themselves to themselves. You went ashore; you'd go ashore with some of your mates from your own mess probably, not even from a different mess. There was very little social contact across the messes. The messes were rather like, I suppose, families on a small estate: they're all part of the estate but it was very much family first. (*Arthur*)

I wouldn't say there was tension. I think the worst part about it was that a lot of the chaps who had been called up were moaning about their lot all the time, which us regulars couldn't do anything about anyway. And nor could they; they were in and that was it. And they were always comparing the amount of wages they got in civilian life to what they were getting in the service, and, of course, that was much more than what we were getting. Some of them had their pay even made up by their civilian firms. But I wouldn't say there was any real tensions, it was just uncomfortable at times. (*Grant*)

People come up and speak to you, as if you'd been there for years sort of. It was a friendly atmosphere. It was different. One bloke was speaking to me, and I didn't know who he was, and I said to someone, 'Who was that?', and he said, 'Oh, he's a Jimmy, the first lieutenant; he comes next one down from the skipper.' And he came and spoke to me and asked me who I was and where I came from, and where I'd been and all that, in a nice manner. He didn't have a hat on; he had shorts on, his shirt hanging out. Now on the *Wye* you weren't allowed on deck without your hat on, you weren't allowed on deck without your lifebelt, you had to take your lifebelt with you all the time – don't matter what you done, you kept your lifebelt with you. On the *Crocus* they never worried, it was a different navy, different navy altogether. And you could go to any part of the ship, any deck, there were no restrictions for officers only or anything like that. (*Jolly*)

Not only that, you had some wonderful officers, who you respected for their rank, but in the end they were gentlemen. I remember one, he was a New Zealander, and if you went up on the bridge during the morning watch, along with him, he'd come along and he'd want to know what you did in

civvy life, whether you were married, whether you had any children, if you knew what they were doing, what you intended to do after you left the Navy. And he'd tell you all that he'd done in New Zealand, and it was almost as though you were talking to your father, as opposed to an officer. Another thing he used to do was that he had a great big sheet of cardboard up on the bridge onto which everyone's name who went up on lookout was put, and you got awarded so many points for spotting an aircraft or a ship signalling in, or probably a raft floating by. And I can always remember him saying that if you spot a submarine and we sink it, he would try and get you the VC. But he was a marvellous, marvellous fellow, and he wouldn't ask you to do anything that he wouldn't do himself.

Cyril Stephens, Colombo, 1945 (*courtesy Cyril Stephens*)

There was that lovely companionship. You know, you were like a big family, wonderful. Bagsy Baker. He was a very good fellow he was. He was all for the lads. But he married one of the musicians from Ivy Benson's band. I can always remember when we were going on the wheel to harbour, he'd look out the wheelhouse door. He wouldn't take much notice of what they were telling him from the bridge, you know, he'd say, 'They don't know what they're doing up there.' But he was a fellow who gave you confidence. This is it. And he'd stick by you through thick and thin. There was no bitterness, you know. I am the great almighty, you know, you do what I say or else. You know, you were led quietly aside and he said, 'Now you don't do things like this.' (*Stephens*)

I think the magic of a 'Flower' class corvette is that it's small, a very close-knit company of a crew and everyone of you have shared the same experiences, the same feelings. And you have the same feelings when you bring survivors on board who can't stand up or are completely unconscious because of their time in the water. The ratings that go ashore and get themselves into trouble with the police, and you go ashore and bail them out or get them out on some excuse or other. It was a family affair. Very much so and it was, it can only be, because we were a small ship. We were always at sea. We were never in harbour long enough for them to become detached, for want of a better word. You'd get into harbour. You'd have about seven days. Half the ship's company would most likely go ashore, on leave, for five of those days if not six, and then you'd come back and you're back at sea again. And when you were in harbour on watch, or on duty all the time whilst the other party were on leave, you were still working with the ship's company. Still getting to do the normal routines of a ship. Because although we were small, and we were manned by reservists and HOs we maintained a routine as good and equal to any destroyer. We prided ourselves on the routine that we carried out. It was proper, like any other ship. (*Dykes*)

'The Same Sort of Danger'

THE MEN AT WORK

Well I think we were all going through the same sort of thing. We were in the same sort of danger, although probably we didn't recognize it as danger at that time, but you were in it together. There was no running away from it, was there? You were there and you had to get on with it.

DRUMMOND

For instance, the navigator, his task was to keep his charts up to date, wherever we might be operating, ensuring that the changes are made and also making sure that he knew where our ship's position was at any given time. It could be difficult because we could have a storm in the Atlantic that could last three or four days, and our position was usually on a dead reckoning basis. That is, you knew that you'd steered a certain course for a period of time, at a certain speed. If you had a very bad wind, you set off its direction against the course that you steered, and that would give you a rough idea of where you were. The only time that you could confirm your position was if you [were able to get a gun sight or a star sight], if you had a clear sky, where you could take a star sight. We had no electronic, not at that time, no electronic ways and means of ascertaining the accuracy of our position. (*Dykes*)

HMS Clematis, *Lieutenant John Horn (left) and Frank Richmond on watch, Newfoundland, 1943* (courtesy Frank Richmond)

One had a job, one observed one's course and speed. Keeping station in itself was a job, was sufficient to keep one awake – particularly at night when one's every sense was alert – not only were there any U-boats about, but also where was the convoy, where was our particular ship, or ships, how were they doing, was there anything going on in the convoy, was there any light showing, so that there was no fear of going to sleep.

One kept visual sighting as far as possible. That meant that one determined one's station by sight, or in fact by smell, if the wind was in the correct direction. Our favourite station was on one quarter or the other of the convoy so that we would not fall foul of stragglers, but we could keep an eye on the convoy as a whole. (*Hollinshed*)

On a watch, it didn't really alter when you became a PO [Petty Officer]. You still had a watch to keep. If there were any panics during the night you would make certain that people had closed up properly. I would check. I went on to the 4-inch gun when I was a PO. When I was a leading hand I went on to the Oerlikon, but if, for instance, a boat was called away for a rescue, when I was the buffer I would be responsible for getting that boat into the water and lowering it and hoisting it. Any survivors that had to be picked up I would have to make certain, for instance, that scrambling nets, life rafts, everything was prepared. I was responsible for all the seamen under me to get on to the job. (*Drummond*)

We looked for any object. Any object in the sea, periscopes mostly, that's what you'd got in your mind. But if you'd see a wooden box you'd report it. You'd report the bearing of it, where it is. Sometimes on the horizon you might see just a speck poking up on the horizon, you might see [an object] just like a stick, you report it. Often the top of a mast of a merchantman, might be neutral ship or anything, but you report everything you see. Or if you see any seagulls, a batch of seagulls circling round something, you report that. Because it could be something in the water there you know, some disturbance in the water. You'd just report anything. It gets boring after a while, but at night you're looking out, you can't see a thing you know, but you're still looking out just the same, just looking into black. (*Jolly*)

Most of the time it was very boring, most of the time you were just waiting and watching and not ever letting up on your concentration, that was the hardest problem. You had binoculars, you were searching the horizon with those binoculars to look for periscopes, or to look for something, and you never let up. And you didn't because you know you had the pressure of knowing there was someone looking for you. (*Arthur*)

Dennis Jolly, Gibraltar, 1945 (courtesy Dennis Jolly)

We were always on the bridge with the yeoman, and a couple of signalmen or leading signalmen, mainly I suppose because you had sixty ships in the convoy and six ships in an escort so one man couldn't have handled the whole lot with signals coming in all the time. And at night-time, of course, we had to make signals all visual because we couldn't use the radio. [We had to use] a little blue light attached to the top of the binoculars, with a little button that you pressed with your small finger on the top [of the lights], and get replies through the whatshisname there.

Most of the signals come from our skipper when he was Captain D, but if you weren't with Captain D's boat, then of course you didn't get so many signals, you know. But we didn't do direct signalling unless you were a Captain D. And when you were Captain D then you always had a couple of extra signalmen on board to take care of it, you know. But it was a bit funny at times, some of the answers you got. And of course a lot of these skippers were foreigners anyway. You know can hardly speak English, let alone signal in English.

In the fog you couldn't see what was going on. It was eerie, too, in thick fog. But you couldn't use RT [Radio Transmission] except in emergencies. If you were actually in action then there was no point in keeping quiet. But normal signalling you couldn't. And then, of course, we were trying to signal to these merchant [ships], who'd never signalled to anybody in their lives you know, and where we were pretty smart in those days, rattling off about twenty words a minute, we had to wait for a minute [for their reply]. (*Donkin*)

There was two major grades of codes and cyphers, these could be decoded by the ratings, specialist ratings. But others could only be decoded by officers. So very often I'd come off after four hours of the bridge and have a signal to decode before I could turn into my bunk. Then you had a lot of [confidential secret code] books. They were continually being changed for security reasons, and you had to account for every one of them. Destroy them and issue a destruction certificate, take on new ones. It was quite an involved business. [We had] a special weighted sack, and one was supposed to get all these books out of the safe. I don't know how one would have done it, but [we had to] get all the books out of the safe, which was held in the captain's cabin, put them in the sack and throw them over the side. I think there would be very little time to do that, quite frankly. (*Richmond*)

When the Yanks came into the war we had to learn a whole lot of codes. New meanings for different flags, and when you were working with them, of course, it was a bit more difficult. But not specifically English changes, mainly to accommodate the allies, I suppose, that sort of thing. (*Donkin*)

[The Radar Direction Finder] was one of these screens where the aerial went backwards and forwards. It didn't revolve like they do now. It was one of the first ones. They did about, I think, half an hour each. There were two of them on duty and they did about half an hour each watching it. And that was long enough apparently. They were on duty, I suppose, four hours, but they did it in half-hour times so that they could cope with it. (*Helen Canham*)

HMS Snowflake, *a working party, Atlantic, 1942* (*courtesy Cyril Hatton*)

I became responsible for everything regarding seamen's duties in that ship. The training of the younger people, responsibility for painting, ship's husbandry. Ship's husbandry would be anchors, cables, all the wire work in the ship, all the rope work in the ship, all the boats, so it was general maintenance, a bit like a housewife really. (*Drummond*)

I started off as an ordinary seaman. You just worked part of the ship you know. Probably washing paintwork, scrubbing paintwork, going on watch. You see you never took on – you'd do a lookout's job, but you wouldn't have a job like helmsman until you were an AB, Able Seaman, which you passed the test for. And then when you went on to the wheel as an Able Seaman, then you'd have the helmsman, or the quartermaster as he'd be called. He'd be with you and he'd shout to the bridge that he was going to let the Able Seaman take the wheel. And he'd stand by you until you got confident that you could handle the thing yourself.

Well, being as I was a decorator, they immediately found out that I'd be just the fellow in charge of the paint store. So my job was to dole out the paint and the brushes and the special job I used to do was to repaint the check funnel. We had black and white check round our funnel, which was the B3 group recognition sign, and also the pennant numbers on the stern and on the bows.

A painting party, Atlantic, 1942 (Royal Naval Museum Collection)

Not a bad job. You never done it in bad weather. But we did once paint ship on the way back from an Atlantic convoy, and this may sound strange to anyone, but that sea that day was as flat as a plate. It's amazing. We had long toms, which is a brush with a long handle on, we leant over the side and painted, and I remember because, when we got into harbour, we got rude remarks from the other ships' crews: 'Get some sea time in.' (*Stephens*)

The [crew] who weren't cook of the mess? [Well] there was always the famous captain of the heads, who was always very specially selected. They tried to make it so only a CW rating was appointed captain of the heads, but most of us had been tipped off beforehand. There was usually some chap who wanted a quiet number, because nobody was going to interrupt him. He was excused from most things. But the rest of the [crew], when the hands fell in in the morning and detailed off to working parties, it was nearly always a chipping hammer or a paint brush, that was at sea, or in harbour, you were chipping off old paint and putting on fresh paint. The whole of the ship would be painted by the seamen. That's the funnel, the hull, everything, continuously. Because it gave them something to do, I suppose, but it also·kept the ship looking fairly clean and neat and tidy. And there were difficult moments when you were covered in paint when you tried to climb up from the stage over the fo'c's'le and try and get back on board and your hands are slipping. That was some of the more exciting moments, I suppose. But most of the time, I think, what we remember was chipping paint and painting. That was a preoccupation. (*Arthur*)

Engine room. There were the old-fashioned merchant-type engines, reciprocating engines, and one propeller, one screw, and what we call the old 'up and downers'. And you had two boilers, and there used to be a stoker on one and a leading stoker on the other. But the leading stoker (there was a doorway between the two

HMS Poppy*, two stokers, Londonderry,* *1944* (*courtesy Ted Kirby*)

boilers, two small boiler rooms), he looked after both boilers, but he had one stoker on the aft boiler usually. Both boilers were managed so it was controlled, usually by a Petty Officer. There was natural ventilation, great big fan intakes. No fans like they have in modern navies. If you were going into wind, you had to get on top and slew this thing round like a gooseneck thing. And that was your ventilation, and if you weren't quick on it and you changed direction, and you shipped the sea, then the stoker and Petty Officer underneath on the controls got wet through, it sheeted down. (*Hallam*)

I used to be what they called the gun-layer. Now he was the chap who moved the gun up and down in elevation. On the right-hand side of the gun was the trainer who moved it left and right. I would look through a telescope, and in the telescope would be a crosswire, and at a target, I would then pull the trigger and the gun would fire. I would then observe where the shell fell, give a correction, which was then placed on the sight by the sight setter. For instance, if I said, 'Up 800 yards', then he put up 800 on the sight, my telescope would be pressed by an angle equal to 800 yards, so I would have to elevate a bit more than what I was previously. In other words the gun would cock up a bit higher. Well, that was my job as the gun-layer. (*Grant*)

CHAPTER TWO

THE CORVETTES
IN CONVOY

The weather was the worst of the lot, and I think any corvette sailor would tell the same thing.

Howard O. Goldsmith, RN, 1939–1946;
Leading Sick-Berth Attendant,
HMS SNOWFLAKE

The need for convoys became apparent as the war progressed and the corvettes, which were initially designed for coastal escort work, were used to escort them across the Atlantic. The war developed as a conflict not only of strategy, but also, importantly, of technology, and the convoys and the corvettes were modified according to the evolving outcome of these factors. Convoys got larger, air support increased, and training and tactics became more sophisticated. Technological developments such as the introduction to the corvettes of the 'Hedgehog', a forward-throwing weapon, the gyro compass, radar and refuelling at sea, along with advances in intelligence, increased efficiency and effectiveness. The crews, although not particularly aware of the larger picture of the war's tactics and strategy, fully appreciated the technological innovations introduced in their ships.

'A Search and Rescue Sheepdog'

THE PATTERNS OF THE CONVOYS

We were a sheepdog, in fact, but also a search and rescue sheepdog in that many stragglers were unfortunately the victims of U-boats, should there be any following the convoy. So that, should a straggler be in difficulties, we had to collect the survivors.

HOLLINSHED

I think [convoys] developed very much on the lines that it was important to supply Great Britain as a base for the allies. The only way to do that was by sea. And all ships, whether they were coming from South Africa or South America or Australia, had to come through that area. The Channel was closed, so everything came north about. And the convoys were routed. At the beginning of the war there were no convoys: there were fast troop ships, etcetera, but there were no convoys. They began forming the convoys; they got more escorts; they got better escorts, better equipment, better trained convoy commodores and ship's masters, better trained escorts. Meantime the U-boats were coming up more, and more and more, and then they of course had St Nazaire as a base, which allowed them to penetrate further into the Atlantic.

Some of [the ships] fuelled at sea. In those early days, in mid-Atlantic, far remote from the regular channels. Later that became extremely difficult because of air cover, but the submarines developed. They got bigger, better

HMS Clematis, *Plymouth, 1942* (*courtesy Frank Richmond*)

fuel-carrying capacities and they were highly trained. As the war went on and more submarines were sunk, they had difficulty replacing the U-boat crews and experienced U-boat commanders. There were one or two very brilliant ones, but they got killed off, most of them. There were very few of them left. And as the war developed and we got better radar, better asdics, air cover, more ships, finally the allies dominated.

Dönitz [Grand Admiral Karl Dönitz, Commander-in-Chief, German Navy] had a great attempt in May '43 with his wolf packs. He had developed the wolf pack technique of having a scout, scouts spread right across the big gap from South Ireland, every so many miles, and the scouts would record or report, not attack a convoy. And several scouts would report that convoy so they would have its route pretty well, and its position. And they developed the technique of having many U-boats in position, ahead of that convoy. And they used to descend upon a convoy, and that is how it developed. And I think finally in May '43, when we had the very decisive battles and B7 was in that decisive battle, his losses by aircraft attack, escort command, escort group attack became so much that he couldn't replace the [submarines] and he certainly couldn't replace the men. So it began to peter out. We had succeeded, and I think – in April, May, June, July '43 – I think Gretton was transferred somewhere else to another theatre of war. The Battle of the Atlantic had been decided. It began to wind down a bit towards the end of '44, but you still had escorts. (*Atkinson*)

HMS Snapdragon, *Ronald James on Twin Lewis guns, en route to Tobruk, 1942*
(*courtesy Ronald James*)

The only air activity we would have would be the Focke-Wulf Kondors, which were four-engine aircraft, reconnaissance aircraft, and their sole task was to home the U-boats on to us and there was not much that we could do about it. We'd fire our guns at it, but it didn't have any effect. If we left the convoy and went at speed out to 4 or 5 miles from the convoy to catch the Kondor as it flew round, it would just fly further away out of gun range. (*Dykes*)

ONS5 – we've subsequently learned that it was probably the turning point of the Battle of the Atlantic, and probably the termination of the Battle of the Atlantic, in so far as we hammered the Germans so hard on that trip, and they did so poorly in sinking our ships, that history records that Dönitz realized that we'd got too good for him. And even the big wolf packs of forty odd U-boats weren't having the impact that they should do, and that they weren't cost effective, either in time, money or men. And I think there were a couple of convoys after that that were quite hairy, but history records that ONS5 was the turning point of the Battle of the Atlantic.

We left 'Derry [Londonderry] at the end of April with forty-two ships. The first contact with U-boats was on the 29th, the day after. The first ship to be sunk was the *McKeesport*, the first merchant ship, and then we finally got to St John's. I haven't got the date we actually arrived, but on May the 28th HMS *Duncan*, which was a destroyer, sank four [U-boats]. We attacked another which fired at us, and I think we sunk her. I don't think it was a positive sinking, but we're pretty sure we sank her, although I don't think we were credited with it. So we must have gone into St John's about the 30th of May. We were at sea a month. We must have been at sea three to four weeks, but only because it was such terrible, terrible weather. Normally I think the longest run was about a fortnight, with a very slow convoy, which sounds ludicrous now, when people are nipping across the Atlantic in a couple of hours. But it just got progressively worse and worse and worse until we got these mountainous seas. I know one merchant ship just broke up and disappeared, and nobody knew what happened to her. It could have been torpedoed, but I doubt it because the sea, I think, was even too bad for the U-boats to attack. The convoy was virtually going backwards at times. It was absolutely atrocious weather, it really was.

But then, as I say, towards the end of the convoy, the weather suddenly calmed for no apparent reason at all. The wind just dropped; the sea flattened out; the fog came down. The U-boats moved in, but so did we. And that was the first chance we had to really have a go at them, because they could operate in weather that we couldn't operate against them. They had the whip hand in bad weather up to a point. Well, then it was our turn, and as I say we put down, I think it was seven, I think we put seven U-boats down in the end between us, and that was it. Old Dönitz didn't like that a bit. He'd decided he'd had enough. (*Goldsmith*)

The convoys were formed as for the last war. Churchill's idea was very much for convoys, and at the beginning of the war there were no convoys, ships

HMS Snowflake, *a 4-inch breach-loading gun, Atlantic, 1943* (*courtesy Cyril Hatton*)

were just picked off, no defence. In convoys you got a number of ships together and, of course, it would be wonderful for a U-boat just to find a lot of ships and just to fire his torpedo loosely into them. So they had to be protected, and therefore you might get four or five corvettes assigned to one convoy. Not a lot. One ahead, perhaps, say two on the sides and one astern. Not a lot of protection. Usually in a group there would be one destroyer, because corvettes had limited speed: they only could do 16 knots – not enough. And you kept at a particular pattern: you either had position a or b or c or d. That was your particular position, and you had to cruise and cruise and cruise around there. They didn't always have a destroyer. Sometimes they had a 'River' class frigate ahead, but sometime they might have a destroyer plus a couple of 'River' class frigates. (*Atkinson*)

There was always a pre-convoy conference where the merchant navy captains and the captains of the escorts met at a meeting. I don't know what actually took place at those sort of meetings, but they would have formed some particular convoy order, maybe three lines, two lines, four lines. They would then have explained how the escort screening would be, and you would follow that particular pattern. But if, for instance, you were leaving Liverpool, the merchant ships would have congregated at some pre-arranged spot and the escorts would have gathered around them, and then they would have proceeded when they'd got that right sort of order in line. The escorts would, as they got more into the open sea, would have a pattern of a zig-zag to cross each other's lines for asdic control. (*Drummond*)

[The convoys got] larger and they themselves were more efficient. Very much larger. You always got stragglers. You get a hundred ships in a convoy, there's always somebody can only go at 7 knots, and the speed of the convoy is the speed of the slowest ship. The strength of a [chain] is the strength of the weakest link. Sometimes you got two or three and one might be detached. One escort might be detached to look after the stragglers, because you could not hold up the whole of the convoy. The captains themselves of the merchant ships were very fine men. They attended the convoy meetings before they left, were given documents, told what position they had to get into and they became very efficient. Don't forget, a convoy of a hundred ships wouldn't start from one port. West bound you'd get a Glasgow section, you'd get a Liverpool section. Each may be five, ten, fifteen ships, and the east coast lot would have escorts and they'd anchor until they all joined, and then they would take position off Rockall, near Ireland, and the Liverpool section would be directed there and the South Wales section. So they built themselves up and slowly got into positions. Each convoy had a commodore, who was in the leading ship, and he managed his hundred ships by visual flag signals. They didn't have walkie-talkies; they weren't allowed to break WT [Wireless Telegraphy] silence, so they had to do it by visual signals. (*Atkinson*)

We were based in Liverpool – Albert Dock to be precise, sometimes Gladstone Dock. After the convoy conference the captain would attend with the navigating officer. We would then wait for our sailing instructions, and we would leave Albert Dock and proceed down the river, down the Mersey, into the swept channel, and following us would come the merchant ships, usually in two columns. It had to be two columns because the swept channel wasn't wide enough for any more columns. Once out of the swept channel in the Irish Sea, the convoy would form up into the appropriate number of columns that were given to those ships. We would proceed through St George's Channel and into the Atlantic. Once we got into the Irish Sea, having taken up our station, which would be set for us by the SO [Senior Officer] of the escort, we would proceed on a normal watch-keeping basis for the rest of the journey. Sometimes we might be joined by ships that had come

HMS Burdock, *c. late 1941, early 1942, after her modification. Note extended fo'c's'le, RDF and Type 271 radar on bridge, foremast abaft bridge, 20 mm guns in bridge wings, 40 mm pom-pom* (courtesy James Goss)

from the Clyde, and they would form up their own columns either to the port or starboard of the existing convoy. There would be no further escorts now that we had the Clyde portion joined, and we would just continue on that basis. (*Dykes*)

Well, what we used to do – we were based at Greenock and so we'd be picking up ships from Loch Ewe, or around that area and we'd assemble just off Scotland and then we'd head towards Halifax. Although St John's was our main [base] where we used to go to. And the speed of the convoy is, of course, the speed of the slowest ship. So if you had a fast convoy, you know, you could do about 9 to 10 knots. You'd have a destroyer who's the escort leader and they'd be in the front and all us corvettes would be round the side, you know on the flanks. There'd be one at the stern, which had a nickname: 'Tail-end Charlie'. If you can imagine a rectangle of ships covering probably 4 or 5 miles and a destroyer at the head of them, and the corvettes at the side would sweep in with their asdic domes and away she'd go. And every so often they'd alter course during the night. All depends what information they got from Admiralty where the U-boats were, so they'd alter course. Providing we had lovely weather the [convoy would] stick fairly well together, but if it became rough, and some of the merchant ships, I reckon, were tied up with string and wire, and they would get behind you see. You'd have to round them up and that was a job for 'Tail-end Charlie'. (*Stephens*)

[At first] we never took the convoy completely over to Halifax or the American ports. Usually the Canadian corvettes used to come out and meet us just off Newfoundland, and we would go into Argentia and the Canadian groups would take the convoy for the rest of the journey. (*Richmond*)

We went over to Nova Scotia. This was our first transatlantic crossing and we found it much easier than transferring to a homeward bound convoy in mid-ocean. And the convoys themselves felt much happier in that, at that time, the mid-Atlantic gap, devoid of air cover, was a very worrying time for the merchant vessel. They regarded that, and quite rightly, as the most dangerous period of the trip.

A group was formed ad hoc for each convoy. Usually a destroyer would be the senior officer and corvettes would be distributed around on each beam and on each quarter. If there were sufficient, there would be one on each bow as well. The corvettes usually on each quarter or astern would be detailed, the following morning, to round up stragglers, chase them back into formation. (*Hollinshed*)

You picked up a convoy at sea. The convoy was already sailing. And you joined your escort group. *Anemone* was in B4 [group], which was painted on the funnel. And your escort group was detailed off to various positions, but as an ordinary seaman, or an able-bodied seaman, you didn't know what the hell was going on and nobody else did. Your job was to do what you were told, which was a very small cog in the machine. So you saw the convoy, but you didn't know how big it was. There were rumours getting around perhaps, maybe twenty, thirty ships. Convoys were very strange because there was the odd straggler that had to be looked after, but convoys were pretty old ships very often. The average speed of a slow convoy, I think, was 6 to 8 knots, which was ludicrous – a lot of hard work getting them across safely. A fast convoy, which was better, was about 12 knots. (*Arthur*)

Usually forty ships: ten columns, four to a column, sometimes bigger, particularly if you had another convoy join. Sometimes we picked up a convoy that was slow moving and they would join us for a while. You would also pick up ships that were straggling from other convoys that had gone in the past. They would also join us. (*Dykes*)

And then, of course, the big saving was eventually when the Coastal Command gave us air cover. And that, of course, made a huge difference because the aircraft could not only spot the U-boats on the surface, because U-boats wouldn't go down unless they had to, but they could also attack them. And if they could come out of the sun, they could very often catch a U-boat completely unawares and just straddle him with bombs and finish him. And that, of course, was an enormous help. It really was. That made life a lot easier. (*Goldsmith*)

Then, of course, the other big thing was air. Once we got the gap and did away with the gap by getting long-range aircraft, there again we cussed Harris who would not release the long-range aircraft. He wanted them all to carry bombs over Europe. They didn't want many. But fortunately the Americans came to the party and loaned us twenty-four, I think, twenty-four long-range Liberators, and that made all the difference in the world – stopped the mobility of the U-boat. He couldn't come steaming up round the convoy by day to get at his position for a night attack. Once you denied him the surface by day, you really clipped his wings. Twenty or so long-range aircraft – twenty aircraft was far more valuable than twenty ships and proved their worth, and, of course, you'd got the carrier groups out there – the escort carrier groups. Their job was to sink U-boats and they did that very effectively. (*Chesterman*)

HMS Snapdragon. *Ronald James (centre) by an A-bracket in the bow. The A-bracket was lowered to search for acoustic mines, 1942 (courtesy Ronald James)*

But basically that's what it would be. We would have a frigate as our escort and we would have three 'Flower' class corvettes and a trawler. Coastal Command would give us air cover. They would stay with us as long as it was feasibly possible for them, because of endurance. We would have the Sunderland flying boats, Hudsons and the Catalina aircraft. They would stay an hour, possibly two hours, and then they would have to leave. But the further west we got the less time these aircraft stayed with us because of endurance problems. (*Dykes*)

The escort, of course, was always continually zig-zagging – not in a regular formation but in an irregular manner, so that if there was a U-boat watching it made it very difficult for him to estimate your direction at any one time. The convoy, of course, proceeded in one direction. They were usually about seven lines across and about four, sometimes five, but about four ships in line, so the average convoy was round about twenty-eight to sometimes thirty-eight ships. Average speed – schedule speed – was slow: 7 knots, and the faster convoys 9 knots.

Generally speaking there were four or five corvettes, plus one and sometimes two destroyers. So usually the destroyer would be zig-zagging across the face of the convoy, and the corvettes would be positioned round each side to keep a continuous asdic screen all round. And maybe also there would be a corvette or maybe a special rescue ship stationed at the stern of the convoy to pick up survivors, if we lost a ship. (*Richmond*)

Our screen was usually a destroyer leading, flanked by other destroyers and corvettes, normally about five, with one for'ard, port for'ard. One port aft, starboard for'ard and starboard aft, on the outsides of all the others [available escorts permitting]. The fifth one did what we called a stern sweep. He was the one, the danger one. ['Tail-end Charlie'] That was a danger, no doubt about that, because he would be astern, doing a stern sweep, up and down all the time. By then the convoy was somewhere about 20 miles ahead of you, well ahead. So you were on your own down there astern. I remember one day it happened to us. We were doing the stern sweep and suddenly a U-boat appeared on the surface, oh, less than 2 miles away. I saw it – three or four of us saw it – didn't believe it. Fairly calm waters, you could see it like a broom handle going through the water. I said, 'Can't be', and suddenly this thing surfaced. I don't know its number, I forgot. And action stations straight away, and the gunners went straight to the gun, four in gun for'ard, and they managed to get one round off for this, missed it. It crash dived and then we went after it, and we stayed with it for a long, long time, pattern after pattern, but we'd had no proof, to my knowledge there's no proof, but I do believe that we got a possible, a possible, out of that one. (*Hallam*)

We knew the number of passengers on the ships. We knew the number of crew. We knew their cargoes. The [information was] given to us at the convoy conference and that information was found on what was known as the convoy form, which was literally a predrawn diagram of the convoy with all the names of the ships in their appropriate positions.

[The ships carried] meat, cereals, lubricating oils, machinery, wood, newspaper or paper pulp, chemicals, iron ore, all forms of minerals, cement. I think pretty well everything under the sun. In fact, the first two or three convoys that I was on it was an experience to realize how this country relied on imports of all types, metal, as I say, iron ore, that you realized exactly how dependent we were to keep the country going. [There were also] military personnel taking up appointments in America, also prisoners of war taken over there by ship and also just civilians coming over, working for the government or whoever it might be, going to Canada or America – women and children of diplomatic staff. (*Dykes*)

Some convoys do remain in one's mind, simply due to the formation, i.e. a very large one or a formation sometimes of very small vessels, who were unwieldy, difficult to manage, difficult to control and, in the bad weather that one had, they behaved in the most peculiar fashion. All ship's masters had firm ideas on how their ships handled in bad weather, and they disliked

HMS Amaranthus, *1942* (*courtesy James Goss*)

intensely being in close company one with another, and they would tend to disperse. They remained in convoy, but [created] a very extended convoy, [so as to give] them sea room. And only when the weather moderated would they attempt to resume their close convoy formation. Ship's masters quite often were optimistic in their assessment of their power and speed. They hoped that in a faster convoy they would be better protected, then in bad weather, of course, they tended to fall astern, slowing the convoy down as a whole. [The corvettes] would move alongside them, urge them to increase to maximum power, and point out that should they remain a straggler they would be in very great danger. This usually had the desired effect of more smoke from the funnel, to which we would say, 'Make less smoke', but eventually they would rejoin the convoy and make a little extra speed. (*Hollinshed*)

If we'd had [support groups] from the beginning we'd never have been losing the millions of tons of ships we lost. There are the two distinct roles. I mean our role was as a close escort, was for the safe and timely arrival of the convoy. We were protecting merchant ships not sinking U-boats. If you could sink a U-boat, good, but you really couldn't afford more than, say, 10 or 15 minutes attacking the U-boat, otherwise you've left your screen open and, while you're busy doing that, in comes a U-boat or two U-boats and knocks off two or three ships. So it was essential to keep the screen intact. Drive the U-boat off, the U-boat that turned away and went down the stern of the convoy. Well, forget him; he won't do any harm. The one that turns and parallels the convoy, well, you've got to chase him, try and make him dive, drop a couple of depth-charges. One pattern of depth-charges, if you can afford it, and forget about him for the night. He won't attack that night. So that was our job. Keep the U-boats from getting at the merchant ships not sinking U-boats. The escort to the support groups, their job was to sink U-boats. They would hunt him to exhaustion. Two or three of the group get one U-boat – kill him and that's what they did, very effective. So there were two distinct roles, but both essential. As I say, we weren't sinking U-boats so there were more and more coming out. Had we had the support groups in the earlier days, then U-boat numbers would have been kept down and would never have reached the peak numbers they did. (*Chesterman*)

Success was not always measured, of course, by sinking of U-boats. Outward bound convoys were probably under ballast, not many of them were laden with cargo. Homeward bound they were laden to the gills with tanks, oil, munitions, food, so it is better to get a ship through if you can. And HX231, which followed ONS5, would probably be one of our most brilliant successes. And although that convoy was attacked and attacked and attacked, I don't think any U-boats were sunk, but no merchant ship was sunk. And I think I'm right in saying something like a 150 ships came through from America, laden to the gills. The convoy stretched 7 miles – you couldn't see the other end of it, and all the ships were brought through by that escort group. No U-boats were sunk – didn't matter, no ships were sunk, so you didn't lose ships and you didn't lose the valuable cargo. (*Atkinson*)

'After the "Hedgehog" Came the "Squid"'

TECHNOLOGICAL DEVELOPMENTS

After the 'Hedgehog' came the 'Squid', which was a much bigger bomb, again fired ahead of the ship, but there were only three Squids to the weapon. A corvette had one weapon of three Squids and they would land ahead of the ship again in a triangle. The Squid was quite an advanced development over the hedgehog, because 5 seconds before the three mortars fired, the depth of the target was automatically set on each of the weapons, each of the bombs. So that you had a very good chance of actually hitting the target.

DYKES

HMS Clover, *starboard, looking aft, 1942. The door open on the right probably belongs to the meat locker, and at the back is a depth-charge thrower* (courtesy David Enright)

When we first commissioned, we had a very, very short fo'c's'le; well, the corvette was based on the trawler, you see. And you came out of the short fo'c's'le into the waist, and to come up into the crow's nest you had to start from the deck and come up, but later on it was altered. Yes, we had that for several years, the short fo'c's'le, then we went to Hull, I think it was Hull when we had the fo'c's'le extended. Well, that meant we had the sick bay come on board then because he had a little caboose of his own, and we had a little tiny canteen and other little stores put alongside. Basically, when we first commissioned we had a very, very short fo'c's'le. (*Stephens*)

We were fitted-out with a 'Hedgehog', that is a forward-firing spigot weapon. The advantage of that was that, whereas you would attack with a depth-charge, you would fire in patterns. You'd have a rough idea of the depth of the U-boat or the target and you'd set your depth-charges accordingly. The first of the pattern would be four depth-charges rolled off the stern at a certain depth, a shallow depth. Then you would have four depth-charges fired, two from each side, from the stalks. They would also be set at a given depth, and then you'd end up that pattern with another four rolled off the stern. So that between the eight charges you hope that you'd get somewhere. But the weakness of that, so far as tactics [were concerned], was that the U-boat commander from their own experience could tell when we were going to drop our charges pretty well, and they could alter course suddenly and they'd be out of the pattern before they exploded. (*Dykes*)

By this time, we had the 'Hedgehog', which projected a small kind of charge ahead. You'd perhaps have twenty-four of them in a pattern, spread out to enclose the submarine. But they had to have contact. They weren't set to go off at a certain depth; they had to touch the submarine. The depth-charge would go off by virtue of the depth to which it [was set], when the primer was set to explode at that particular depth. Later, we got what are called the 'Squid', which was wonderful, which could project the equivalent of a depth-charge about 200 or 300 feet ahead of you. So the first a submarine might know is that he would have explosives raining down on him when you are some distance from him, you didn't have to come and go over him. And then, of course, by that time we all had autoradar – that was crucial. They became astonished by the fact that, whilst these submarines were operating on the surface, which they did because they had to have fresh air and charge their batteries at night, they could be located. And then, of course, later, in '42 and '43, we had aircraft protection flying from Newfoundland, flying from Iceland, flying from bases in Greenland and Northern Ireland. And until then, until about '42, there was the gap in the middle which the aircraft couldn't reach, and that is where the wolf packs lay in wait. So the whole thing developed and there were developments in both sides, but apart from '41, '42, where they had the ascendancy, we later took the ascendancy by virtue of better asdics, good radar and aircraft protection. (*Atkinson*)

With the asdic which was the submarine detection device, you lost contact with a submarine a few hundred yards before you got to it. So when it came to firing your depth-charges, you were more or less firing blind, because between that interval, when you reached the point where you last had a contact, the submarine might have gone anywhere. Might have gone deeper, might have turned to port or starboard, so it was a very hit-and-miss affair. But with the 'Hedgehog' you were able to throw these mortars (there were twenty-four of them), and I think they each weighed about 60 pounds, or something like that. In the [nose] of them they had an impeller, which as they dropped into the water the impeller rotated and armed the mortar, and then if they hit the submarine they exploded – that was the theory. And, of course, as they fired they spread out into quite a big pattern. So there was quite a good chance of hitting the submarine while you were still in contact with it, which was very important. (*Richmond*)

HMS Snowflake, *ready to load depth-charge, Atlantic, 1943* (*courtsey Cyril Hatton*)

When we first commissioned we had the little magnetic compass. There was North-north-east, North-east, East-by-East and you steered by that. You see you had a line which represented the ship's head, and provided she swung the same degrees either side of the ship's head you were more or less on course, but it was very hard going. And I also remember we had the telegraph here, on your right-hand side as you face for'ard, and on the left was a stanchion to which a bucket was attached to be sick in – oh, it was awful. (*Stephens*)

Well, previously we merely had a magnetic compass, and you [found] your way. These compasses have to be corrected very often; they have errors. But with a gyro compass you have the precision and you need a gyro compass to operate your radar properly, to give a correct bearing and report the bearing of an echo that you might obtain. So the gyro compass helped very much in part of the precision under which we had to operate. The coordination of all these instruments – echo sounders, radar, direction finding – you really had to have a gyro compass to be correct. (*Atkinson*)

The gyro, once operating, maintained its course and would not be defected by motion or magnetic influences, whatever. The only slight difference we had with the gyro, was in very northern latitudes, when it tended to be a little suspect, but soon regained its correct bearing when we moved south again. But course and speed in the northern latitude was very difficult. (*Hollinshed*)

Well, [the gyro compass] was, of course, a magnificent aid, because prior to [our] Devonport refit we were relying on a magnetic compass. But with the introduction of the 'Hedgehog', the gyro compass was vitally necessary, so this was a great aid and great improvement. (*Richmond*)

When I first joined the *Honeysuckle* we had magnetic compasses, and then they installed a gyro compass, which was a great asset for us. Naturally, we had our problems with the gyro compasses. They would stop at times, like any electrical equipment. On the other side of it, radar was our first great invention. And the first one that was installed on the *Honeysuckle* was a very small screen about 12 inches wide, and was operated by a small aerial which was revolved by the radar operator turning a handle, so you had a pretty Heath Robinson situation on a very long pole, this handle like a bicycle pedal, and a bicycle chain going up the length of the pole onto the aerial and revolving it in that manner. It worked alright but the type of screen you had was such that we had what was called 'grass', which was at the bottom of the screen. All echoes which were close to the ship would disappear into this grass, which was just a green moving wave at the bottom, so [a target] about

HMS Oxlip, *John Hollinshed (left) and William Leadbetter (captain), c. 1943*
(*courtesy John Hollinshed*)

a mile or so, or 2 miles [distant], you couldn't pick the echo up. And also from the point of view of the Germans, when you picked a submarine up on the surface, naturally the radar operator would hold the target by not revolving his aerial, and in doing so disclose to the U-boat that he'd been picked up, since a U-boat could pick your transmission up. So the next step to that was the continuous revolving aerial, with a round screen as we know it today. So the aerial would be continuously revolving, the echo would be continuously on the screen and the U-boat wouldn't be aware that we could see him. (*Dykes*)

It was 1940 [when it] became essential for microwave radar (that's very short wavelengths), which has the characteristic of staying low along the surface of the sea and therefore right for the detection of targets, near or on the surface of the sea. In this case, of course, the important target was the submarine. The first [centrimetric radar] was taken up to Greenock by some of the team working on it and fitted in the 'Flower' class corvette HMS *Orchis*. It went to trials at sea, which were successful, [although] not as successful as we'd hoped from the beginning. There were reasons for that which we found out later, but nevertheless it produced ranges which were of great use against submarines – far better than anything we'd had before. That doesn't sound very much, but it was about 2 or 3 miles, which in later service came out to 4 or 5 miles on the surfaced submarine, which, of course, is more than you want for an attack. (*Wright*)

HMS Snowflake. *The crew test-launch a kite used to deter attacks from low-flying enemy aircraft,* c. *1942 (courtesy George Ambler)*

The radar was a tremendous boon, because prior to that it must have been extremely difficult – you were really relying purely on sight alone. (*Richmond*)

We went round passed Scapa Flow into Newcastle, into Tyne Dock, where we had a refit for, I think it was six weeks – where they extended the fo'c's'le and added radar. Now we didn't know anything about radar, but when we had the radar it gave us a totally different dimension. It meant that you had radar scan – you could 'see'. You didn't have to have binoculars, you could see at night, you didn't have to get echoes off the surface, you could do your station keeping by radar, you could look for periscopes or U-boats by radar, so you had a great deal more confidence. You weren't any more powerfully armed but you could see better in the dark, and that was great. And, of course, living was more comfortable. You could get your food to the mess without being drowned. We had extra crew and we even had a little sick bay, [including] a sick-berth attendant, which was quite a good idea, because it meant that when we did pick [survivors] up they could be looked after a little bit better. But altogether, when the corvette had that refit, and extended the fo'c's'le, and added the radar, it became a much more effective fighting vessel. And you felt that yourself. It was more comfortable in many ways. (*Arthur*)

We looked forward to having this radar system because we hoped it would ease our station-keeping abilities, particularly at night, [because previously it had been] quite difficult keeping a station in the Atlantic at night, in poor visibility. One had to creep in to the convoy and see if it was still there and whether we were in position, and we hoped that the radar would assist us in this. But, unfortunately, the early radar was very primitive. The operator had to hand operate a very small handle, peaks would appear on a very, very small screen and there was no indication of what these peaks were or what they represented. And we would get, or the operator would perceive, peaks from waves, ships or whatever. There were no means of distinguishing, as far as I could see, between one and the other. And only in the very smooth ocean could one determine that these were actually ships afloat. (*Hollinshed*)

[Radar] more or less did away with lookouts. We were quite obsessed when we had it on board. It was a funny little thing. They stuck 'em on top of the wheelhouse, you know. We thought, what the devil's this thing. And it was this radar, and we had different operators for these [known as] a radar operator. (*Stephens*)

The [U-boats] used to follow you on the surface after dark and submerge in daytime. That was until we got radar. About the seventeenth day out,

HMS Orchis, *North Atlantic convoy (painting by Terry Rogers, courtesy Cyril Stephens and*
Terry Rogers)

everybody would be sort of listening in the wheelhouse to find out where we
were going, because in the wheelhouse there was the wireless cabin, and the
'Sparks' there would be the first one to know, and we would know on the
mess-deck before anyone on the bridge did almost. And you were praying it
would be Halifax. That was the place to be. And they were all talking about
the ice-cream parlours where the girls leant over and picked the ice-cream
out, you know, the whole sailors' dream of heaven. But usually we went to
Argentia. (*Arthur*)

[Refuelling at sea] was another change. The first eighteen months of the war
we could only escort convoys out to 26 degrees west, which was pretty well
due south of Iceland, because of our endurance, and having reached 26
degrees west we would leave the convoy and proceed to Iceland, and wait a
few days and come back with an eastbound convoy. Then they thought up the
idea of oiling at sea, the result of that being that we could then go straight
across the Atlantic to Halifax or to St John's, fuelling once at sea. And, of
course, it had the great advantage of when you did get two or three nights of
sustained U-boat attack you weren't in danger of running out of fuel. We did
that twice. Before we refuelled at sea we became very short of fuel [on two
occasions] because of activities in the night-time and we had to leave the

Oiling at sea, North Atlantic, late 1941
(*courtesy Dick Dykes*)

convoy to go to Iceland to refuel. That's the sort of situation we had, but when we had refuelling facilities at sea, the tanker was always with us. And, when we were short, we just oiled. How they did it – not like your oilers of today with their derricks and various other forms of equipment for oiling alongside – all the tanker did was to trail a wooden float astern, and attached to the wooden float would be a line, and a heavier line would be attached to that. And at the end of that heavier line, possibly a wire, would be the 4-inch or 6-inch hose. And we had to pick up the float with our grappling hook, get it on board, pull up the hose and then connect it to the oiling facility on the fo'c's'le. That was quite difficult in a swell, with the ship rolling and pitching, particularly pitching, because the poor stoker more than once, having got the end of the hose to his chest as he went to connect it to our inlet, would find himself covered in fuel oil as it had choked back through the pipe. But that was the way it was done. (*Dykes*)

Refuelling at sea always used to happen on a Sunday. I don't know why. God, I'd think, I don't know why, it's a fascinating effort. What we used to do. We used to go up to the tanker, get astern of the tanker who let out a manilla rope. You would get onto the fo'c's'le with grappling irons and grapple round this manilla rope. Once you had it you got it inboard, you see, and then the tanker payed out a wire line for us to put on the capstan and then they'd pay out the hosepipe, and the stokers would connect up the oil pipe and they'd pump the oil. But it always used to happen on a Sunday.

[Accidents!] Oh crikey, yes, oil all over the place if one of the couplings came off. But that was more or less the stoker's domain that was. We were up on the fo'c's'le to grapple with the line and the hosepipe. (*Stephens*)

The old method, the ones we used in corvettes, was the streamer pellet buoy down on a light line. We would grapple it up, take it through the bullring, right at the for'ard end of the ship, haul through onto a much stouter line and eventually the oil fuel line would come and you'd take that to a connection, which was just a bit above the fo'c's'le. It was a bit of a difficult operation because the corvette was bouncing up and down. In bad weather it was. There had been one or two occasions when the oil hoses had burst and you'd got all this fuel all over you which can have quite a painful effect to your eyes. That never changed during my time in corvettes at all. And we would probably be taking on fuel then, probably doing 8 knots, not a particularly high speed. (*Drummond*)

Lots of training, lots of courses. When we came into harbour I always made sure that our officers had a two- or a three-day course in signals or the latest radar theme or the latest tactical courses. We just didn't relax. And, of course, we drilled every day at sea, in the dog watches, every day, action stations, drill, drill, drill. Well, every man knew his position and could go there in the dark or any weather and he knew exactly what to do. (*Atkinson*)

And, of course, drill. Many of them became better seamen. They became experienced sailors. Don't forget many of these men had not been to sea before, and after a couple of years or a year they were trained. Also the officers. We had North Atlantic Training Tactical School, under Admiral Sir Max Horton [Commander-in-Chief, Western Approaches], in Liverpool. Fantastic courses on radar, asdics, tactical. Model assistance where they portray a convoy and certain actions happened and you had to immediately give the signals and your reaction and your decisions, and they would point out where you were wrong. So we became a highly trained force. Most of it, of course, by brilliant leadership by Admiral Sir Max Horton and Commodore 'Shrimp' Simpson [G.W.G. Simpson, Commodore (D) Western Approaches] in Northern Ireland. These men became very systematic. When the convoy was over, you came into your base, there was immediately a meeting of commanding officers and officers. What went wrong, whose radar was wrong, any problem with engines, etcetera. And courses of instruction and drill, new inventions – all these things were brought in, and I think that by '42, '43 we were seeing the projection of gyro compasses. It was a highly trained force. Brilliant leadership again, by a fine admiral. (*Atkinson*)

We had a 4-inch breach loading gun, a single pom-pom on the after-deck just up aft of the funnel. In the early days we had two strip Lewis machine-guns, one either side of the bridge, but later they were replaced by Oerlikon guns.

HMS Honeysuckle. *Dick Dykes (left) on Holman's Projector to fire hand-grenades against dive-bombers, 1941* (courtesy Dick Dykes)

We had, roughly speaking, about forty depth-charges. We would have two throwers either side in the waist and then two rails containing depth-charges, so if you wanted to drop some charges you could drop four from your carriers and six from your after rails. That was it – not a lot. (*Drummond*)

We had other small items. We had such a thing as the Holman's projector, which was the most dangerous weapon I've ever come across, because all it was was a mortar, equivalent to a drainpipe, about the same diameter as a drainpipe, fixed to a tank at the bottom, which gave you either compressed air or compressed steam, operated from the ships that supply compressed steam. And you had hand-grenades, held in a metal canister, and they had a 2[½] second fuse, and the object of the exercise was that you pulled the pin out of the hand-grenade and slid the hand-grenade with its canister down the barrel, and the operator of the gun or mortar would fire it at dive-bombers. That was all very well, unless you found that you hadn't got the correct pressure of steam, the result being that the bomb could spill out of the barrel and drop on the deck, and when it's between the potato locker and the beef screen, and one or two other pieces of equipment up there, it would have been a very difficult situation to run away from it. So we disposed of that one very quickly. We never used it, in fact. It was very good for firing potatoes out of. They went for miles in the air. (*Dykes*)

HMS Polyanthus, *the 4-inch gun crew, Atlantic, 1942* (*courtesy Richard Grant*)

We were aware at one time, when the Germans introduced acoustic torpedoes, that their aim was to silence the escorts. But escorts were then provided with what were called 'Foxer', which was a metal contraption towed astern, and by making a noise attracted the acoustic torpedo to this apparatus. And once that was towed astern, I don't think the ship's companies paid much attention to acoustic torpedoes. They were successful on one or two occasions. (Hollinshed) In the *Rhododendron* [an early 'Flower' class corvette, launched on 2 September 1940] we got an echo, we attacked it and it was all over in 30 minutes. In the *Tintagel Castle* [a later 'Castle' class corvette, launched 13 December 1943] we got that contact at half-past five one night. We didn't sink that U-boat till six o'clock the next morning. Now that was doggedness and perseverance by the U-boat and by myself, in that he was very alert. He was a very experienced man. He kept turning. We dogged him. We didn't attack, we waited. We attacked and we stopped. We had limited ammunition on board, and it went on, and we probably followed him for an hour during the night. He probably thought he was away. We were trailing him. Finally we would even attack him at change of watch when their crews were changing. We knew they would be changing at four o'clock in the morning, and finally, about half-past six in the morning, at daylight, we went in and finally . . . we had damaged him during the night, and finally, about half-past six in the morning, we closed in and attacked him and got him. Now that's a long time to keep your concentration going and that is how the war developed. People were better at it, more experienced, better equipment. (*Atkinson*)

We had boffins allocated to us. They were useful people. Peculiar people, but they came up with the right answer. Scientist, you know the crazy scientist. We would have a problem and, you know, we couldn't come up with an answer and you'd tell these blokes, and 'Ah, yes', and they'd disappear, and they'd put the thinking cap on and come up with an answer – most peculiar answers but they did get the answer. Whereas the Germans, the scientists weren't allowed near them, keep them away. They suffered, where we had the advantage. We got a lot of these blokes. They were peculiar blokes to a sailor. I mean, we were practical, logical; they were not. They were quite strange beasts to us – awfully nice fellows, but they produced the answers. Well, silly little things like, you can't read the signal book at night without getting a torch and, 'Well, that's no problem, put it on a strip, put it on a couple of rollers, have a little bit of dull light there and just wind it through.' We'd never have thought of that. Simple things which they could think of. (*Chesterman*)

I don't think many people knew about Ultra or the Enigma machine. Most of us had to find out about that after the war. That was terribly important, of

HMS Orchis, *the ship's company, c. 1943. Cyril Stephens is in the back row, third from right* (*courtesy Cyril Stephens*)

course, and taken in conjunction with the detection devices which we had made a tremendous difference to the submarine war. (*Wright*)

We didn't know anything about [Enigma] till long after the war. One heard rumours that the Germans were breaking our code and that we were breaking their code, but I'm afraid that we didn't see much of it. (*Chesterman*)

But it also made a big difference when our chaps got hold of the Enigma, the German decoding machine, because up to then we couldn't break their code, so we didn't know what they were doing, but they'd broken our codes and they knew exactly what we were doing, and where we were going. But that helped when we got that, because then we had a better idea of what they were up to. (*Goldsmith*)

Well, I remember once getting a fantastic signal. I will give you an example: in HMS *Pink*. We were about 150 miles west-south-west of Iceland, approaching Greenland, and there was a moonlight night – going to be a moonlight night, a very nasty night, windy. And we received a signal from the Commander-in-Chief: 'You may expect attack from down moon at approximately 0200.' Now they knew and were able to interpret in Whitehall the various radio activity and signals by the German U-boats – great activity. They knew where the moon would be and when it would rise and where the U-boat might attack from. And by the feverish increased activity of the radio signalling, they knew attacks were imminent. Now we didn't know that, of course, but the fact that we had a signal telling us to be ready for attack about 0200 made all the difference.

   Admiral Gretton, who was Commander Gretton then, we were so highly trained he sent a signal round to our escort group, and do you know what that signal said? One word – 'Anticipate', that's all he said. Didn't get excited and didn't tell the men to do this or not do the other. It wouldn't have been any good. We were trained; we knew what to do. And do you know what I did? It was about five o'clock, pitch black, windy as hell and I said, 'Hands to tea, six o'clock.' Cleared lower deck and said, 'There's going to be a hell of a battle tonight, I'm not sure how many of us will see daylight. I intend to see it if I can.' So it was up to us. 'We'll pipe down at six-thirty and we'll have action stations at one o'clock, and that means putting on all your Arctic clothing under there and waiting.' Well, some slept and some didn't sleep, but we were there, action stations, at one o'clock. You could almost set an alarm by it. Within a few minutes of two o'clock those attacks began. And I do recall on that terrible, terrible night something like, I think, eighteen ships in that convoy were sunk and something like five U-boats were sunk. They dogged us. And it was after that, that was the convoy [ONS5], that Admiral Dönitz couldn't stand those losses. He hadn't the trained crews to replace and he withdrew. (*Atkinson*)

CHAPTER THREE

AGAINST THE ODDS

If the weather was very bad then you didn't get attacked by submarines.

Richard K. Grant, RN, 1939–1967;
Gunner, HMS POLYANTHUS

The odds against the corvettes and their crews were immense. The weather was often as strident a foe as the U-boat. The interviewees remember that, although the weather in the Atlantic could be nice, for the most part it was rough. Gale-force winds, turbulent seas, cold, rain and, in winter, ice and snow compounded difficulties. Sometimes the gales and seas were so tempestuous that no headway was made. The formal enemy they recall not so much in terms of attacks on themselves but rather in terms of what they did when they went to action stations and the bravery of the survivors, most of whom were merchant seamen. The corvette crews showed great respect for the men of the Merchant Navy. Such respect was not surprising given the terrible conditions the Merchant seamen had to endure if they were unlucky enough to be hit. Consequently, it is on the state of the survivors that the crews dwell – their cries, their conditions when rescued when they were covered in oil, frequently with serious injuries like burns or broken limbs. Often they recollect their sheer helplessness to do no more than what they could, and their lament to this day that they often were unable to rescue all those who survived the initial attacks.

'The Sea That's Following'

WEATHER IN THE NORTH ATLANTIC

In heavy weather, the sea that's following you is higher than the mast of a corvette, so you're in a trough, and when you ride up on that it seems a very funny feeling like going up in a lift, and you get to the top, briefly look around and you see the other ships, and you go down again. So rough weather in a corvette is a fairly lonely experience.

ARTHUR

The weather was atrocious. One gale followed another and yet you could get some beautiful summer evenings, the sea was calm, no wind and beautiful sunsets, and in the winter it really was winter and, of course, it played havoc with the convoy because the ships would scatter from their appointed position in the columns. They had to keep up as much as possible the speed of the convoy. If they straggled then they were left on their own and they had to find their own way to the UK, or whatever port they were going to. They would have a stragglers' route given to them at the convoy conference, but that was up to them. (*Dykes*)

HMS Clover, *lifeboat, starboard side, Atlantic, 1942* (courtesy David Enright)

At one stage, we were north of Iceland actually, HMS *Pink* was detached on one occasion to go on what they call the 'White Patrol', that meant we had to go to Iceland and oscillate between the ice of Greenland and the north-west Cape of Iceland. The fleet was at anchor, under immediate notice, with two anchors down, and the wind was strong. I think the winds were something like, probably, 120, 140 miles an hour. You could be blown overboard. We had to put lifelines fore and aft. And I remember our job – it was in winter, it was dark day and night, no daylight at all – so what with the ice, the whole of the fo'c's'le, the deck, would be thick with ice, and the gun unusable – thick with ice. We were detached to report any radar contact, and when I said, 'Well, what did that mean?', 'Well, we want small ships out there; they can't be seen. And you report any radar contact whatever. It might be the *Bismarck*, we're expecting her to come out.' 'Well, if we report the *Bismarck*, what happens to us?', and the naval officer in charge said, 'We have no plans for you.' Charming. We would have been blown out of the water with our little peashooter, you see. I think that was probably the most severe physical conditions I've ever experienced. (*Atkinson*)

They were so fierce that there were no waves, it was just as if the sea was covered with snow. The waves had been blown into a foam, which was lying and skimming across the surface of the sea. The wind would take the ship and

Ice on HMS Anemone, *December 1942*
(courtesy Edgar Pomeroy)

roll it from one side to the other. [It was] difficult for you to stand up because you'd get into the trough of the sea and you could roll badly and stay over one side before the next wave came to you. (*Dykes*)

The weather was so bad, and there were times there when the convoy was literally stationary because some of the merchant ships just couldn't make headway against the wind and the sea. And although the engines were turning, the screws were turning, we were just sitting there stationary. And to give you an idea of what it was like, the upper deck was out of bounds. The skipper put the upper deck completely out of bounds. The only people allowed above decks were the bridge crew, and they were told to use the captain's companion way, which was inboard to get to the bridge, otherwise out of bounds completely.

People don't realize the tremendous power of the sea, unless you've seen what it can do. But I mean, for instance, all the fo'c's'le stanchions, which were inch-thick iron stanchions, carrying the guard wires round the fo'c's'le, they were all bent at right angles to the deck. They'd just been as though a giant hammer had hammered them over to a right angle. One ship's boat had completely disappeared. One was stoved in. Just the waves had stoved it in, smashed it in. We used to have meat lockers which were welded to the deck. They were on the upper deck to keep the meat fresh, no fridges you see, and they were welded on the deck and to a superstructure above the deck, welded top and bottom, with wire mesh sides to them, so that the air could flow through, and after that storm, not only had they gone, all the meat had gone, and there were just the weld spots on the deck and above, that's all that was left. That's just the force of the wind, the force of the sea, carried all that away. Deck lockers that were bolted and welded down just disappeared, just went, we never saw them go. Incredible power. (*Goldsmith*)

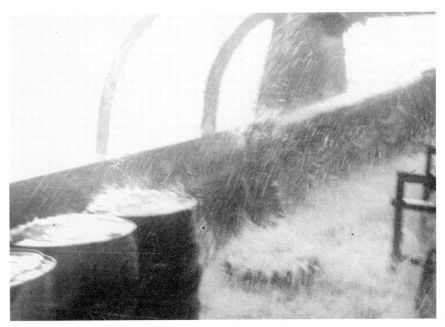

HMS Clover, *looking after for'ard portside, Atlantic, 1942* (*courtesy David Enright*)

The only trouble with the bad weather, except for being so uncomfortable, was the old merchant ships used to tend to break down. They'd drop astern and very often one of the escorts would have to go and try and shivvy them along, or even look after them, if they had valuable cargo on board. But sometimes, of course, the convoy had to take preference, and the ship just straggled along behind the best it could. (*Grant*)

The wind would increase to 50, 60, 70 or 80 knots. The swell would increase to such an extent that it was virtually impossible to make headway. And one would hear, as the ships moved around, crockery and sundry items being broken around the ship as we moved. And sprains and broken limbs were, if not normal, not uncommon. (*Hollinshed*)

It was so bad that most of the crockery was broken. In other words, there were very few plates, hardly any cups. The main thing that the chaps were worried about, or I was worried about, was the rum ration. We used to flatten the round tins of cigarettes – Players twenty-five cigarettes they used to call them. It was an ideal vessel [from which] to drink a tot of rum or have a cup of tea, if you felt like drinking your rum. I always said I was a very good sailor, hardly ever seasick, but there wasn't a man Jack who wasn't seasick on that run; it was terrible. (*James*)

Pack ice outside St John's, Newfoundland, 1945 (courtesy Ted Kirby)

It depended on the sea conditions as to whether it was a regular roll and pitch, because you had the pitch as well as the roll from side to side, and you had the pitch from stern to bow. And it depended very much on the conditions of the sea, as to whether you had a nice gentle roll, which was very rarely, or whether you had a combination of this screwing action of a pitch and toss or roll, which was quite interesting at times. You really had to be extremely careful going up gangways and ladders and things to hold on, because you never knew, and I mean the depth-charge throwers were in the stern, of course, and when you went to action stations, the crew had to go along the exposed deck and it was extremely dangerous. I mean we had lifelines rigged on either side, but the seas used to come in over that and they could easily be swept away. Fortunately, we didn't have that experience but I know ships that did. (*Richmond*)

Well, there were rails and also a rope to hold on to. Well, you had to hang on for grim death, literally, really. And it was hard, I mean to climb up to the bridge from the wardroom by three flights of stairs or ladders, two of which were exposed, and it was really sometimes hard work to climb up the ladder to get to the bridge because of the sheer movement of the boat. And, of course, you'd have spray washing over you all the time. And very often in bad weather the spray would come over the bow and over the bridge, that's why we were so carefully wrapped to try and keep dry. (*Stephens*)

We had one convoy when we got all iced up and we spent hours and hours and hours chipping ice, day and night. It's very, very frightening because a ship rolls and it rolls over and you think it's never going to get back up again. That's frightening, that is frightening. It rolls over to port and starboard and comes back again and you think, is it going to come back up again? (*Stephens*)

But it wasn't all rough weather, some of it was very nice. But when the weather was nice it was absolutely superb, because it was clear sky, and you could see the cumulus clouds going curved over the horizon and you really could see the curve of the earth from the underneath of the cumulus clouds. (*Arthur*)

HMS Oxlip, *off Greenland, 1943* (*courtesy John Hollinshed*)

'*A Dull Thud*'

ATTACKS

Well, the first indication you would have that an attack had started would be a dull thud. At first you'd think that it was an escort dropping depth-charges; it could be. Perhaps he'd got a contact and he was making an attack on this contact. On the other hand, it could be a ship that had just been torpedoed, and then you'd start receiving signals from the senior officer or another corvette where they were reporting that a ship had been attacked.

DYKES

Generally speaking attacks started by being sighted by Focke-Wulf Kondors, that seemed to be the general sort of plan, certainly in the earlier days, 1941. And that

10 Nazis Subs Destroyed In Convoy Attack

Attacks And Counter-Attacks Extended Intermittently Over 8 Days And Nights

ENEMY LAUNCHED THIRTY ATTACKS IN ALL

LONDON, May 12, (Reuters)—An Admiralty communique to-night, Wednesday, states: "Escort ships of the Royal Navy, in cooperation with planes of the Royal Canadian Airforce, have successfully defended a westbound Atlantic convoy against a series of determined and sustained attacks by powerful forces of U-Boats. The attacks and counter-attacks extended intermittently over eight days and nights.

In the last days of April a pack of some eight U-Boats were concentrated on this convoy. A series of attacks were made the majority of which were successfully driven off. On May 1st, it started to blow a gale and this weather lasted for three days. As the weather moderated further U-Boats were concentrated by the enemy and during the 4th., 5th. and 6th., of May it is estimated our escorts were in action with a pack of some twenty-five U-boats. The enemy pressed home his assaults by day and by night in a series of some thirty attacks, and our escorts, in weather which was too heavy for complete air cover, attacked the enemy with determination and success. Two U-Boats were rammed, one by destroyer, the Oribi, Lieut. Commander P. C, A. Ingram, and the other by the Corvette, Sunflower, Lieut. Commander J. Plumer. Another Corvette, the Snowflake, attacked and destroyed a third enemy submarine with depth charges. The fourth U-Boat was sunk by the destroyer Vidette with depth charges.

Aircraft of the Royal Canadian Air Force joined in the battle and carried out many attacks on the U-Boats very probably destroying one and possibly destroying another. Meanwhile and almost without pause escort ships of the Royal Navy continued to harass the enemy. The Corvette Loosestrife attacked a U-boat with depth charges forcing her to the

Trade Dispute Board Named For Bell Island

To Settle Dispute Between Dosco And Employees

Tuesday's Newfoundland Gazette contains the announcement of the appointment by Sir Wilfrid Woods, Commissioner for Public Utilities, of Hon Mr. Justice Dunfield, chairman, Mr. G. P. Bradney and Mr. T. A. Hall, C.B.E. as a Trade Dispute Board for the settlement of a trade dispute between the Dominion Steel and Coal Corporation Ltd., and its workmen at Wabana, represented by the Wabana Mine Workers Union.

The terms of reference are for settlement of the dispute by determining:

(a) what rates of wages shall be paid by the Dominion Steel and Coal Corporation Limited to workmen in the various classes of labour or employment at Wabana Mines Bell Island

From the front page of Newfoundland's Daily News, *Thursday 13 May 1943* (Royal Naval Museum Collection)

then was followed by submarines being homed in to you, usually your first knowledge of that was by someone being torpedoed. (*Drummond*)

When you knew [someone was being attacked] you might be lucky to know where the ship was when it was attacked, that is the number of the ship, so that you could pin-point it in its column in the position of the convoy, but that wasn't always possible, particularly at night. It was just a ship that had been hit, and it was only subsequently that you would discover where it would have been in the convoy. Once you got that attack there were various drills, but the principal drill was [that] each corvette would alter course and steer away from the convoy, leave it and fire, what we called, 'Snowflakes', which really were parachute snow flares which would light up the area in case there was a U-boat on the surface. But then it was a diligent watch on asdics for either the noise of torpedoes or the submarines themselves; you'd pick them up as a contact. And then it was a case of if you've picked up a contact you'd attack it; you don't wait for anyone else to come and help you. You'd attack it with depth-charges. If it was on the surface you'd ram it, no second thoughts about it. And that was done quite a number of times. And that is the way the evening and the night would progress until the next morning, when the attack would finish at daylight. You might get an occasional attack in daylight, but night-time was the main source of activity. (*Dykes*)

If submarines did not send any signals then of course we'd be quite unaware of either a, their existence, or b, their position. Later destroyers had DF [Direction Finder] installations, and if submarines did send signals and they happened to be adjacent to the convoy, the direction could be determined by convoy escorts. And escorts then would be sent to this position to attempt to find them, and put them down. If not sink them, at least deter them from approaching the convoy. But submarines quite often would detect a convoy, shadow, from well astern, hull down, await nightfall and then regain position in order to attack. There were attacks quite often. If the attack was on the far side of the convoy, although we would be of course aware of this and active, the attack would be confined to that side of the convoy and we would take no active part. Similarly, if an attack was on our side, the escorts on the far side of the convoy, whilst alert, would not take an active part, but would be aware of the attack taking place. (*Hollinshed*)

You were lined up each morning for your jobs. You see you served your watches – you did four hours on, eight hours off – and your duty when you're on watch was as a lookout. You would man the guns, man the depth-charges at action stations, but most of the time the corvette was there looking for something. When I first joined, it didn't have any radar. It had the asdic, which was this

HMS Campion, *depth-charge exploding, Atlantic, 1941* (*courtesy Geoff Drummond*)

general ping! ping!, which went on all the time. And the thing that you were expecting to hear when you found a submarine was the [asdic] that went ping! pick!, and there was an echo – [it] galvanized the whole ship. Everybody was waiting for it. Everybody jumped into their action stations.

My action station was on one of the depth-charges, throwers. I think it was a siren that went off when they wanted to fire depth-charges. On the bridge they pushed a button and it made a great noise, and you pushed a button and the thing went phoom! And it blew out this mortar with the depth-charge. And when that went you loaded another one, which was all very well except that the ship was rolling and pitching and they were quite heavy and you had to go through the routine of arming the depth-charges. A depth-charge has a hole in the middle, into which you slide the [pistol and] detonator and you armed it, which means that when it goes over the side it will explode at a preset depth. So you have to . . . you're told at which depth setting to go. Then you arm it and when it fires over the side, then it sinks to that level, and at that level it explodes, by which time you are fortunately some way away. (*Arthur*)

Once action stations had been sounded, we'd take up our positions against the depth-charges. There'd be two ratings on the stern to operate the depth-charge rails, and two ratings on the port and two ratings on the starboard side operating the mortars, that is the depth-charges fired from the stalks. Now as soon as we

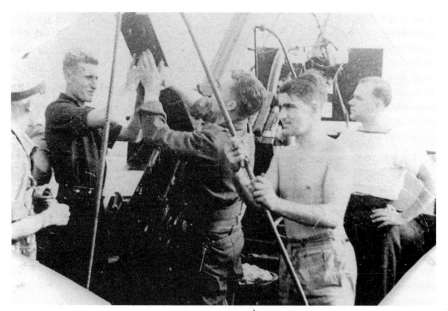

HMS Snapdragon, *Ronald James (centre) on a single pom-pom, 1942* (courtesy Ronald James)

took up action stations we would prime the depth-charges by pushing the primer right through the centre of the charge itself. We would wait at that point for the setting, that is the depth that we had to set on to the pistol of the depth-charge, and that setting would be the depth that they were to explode. Now after that we would wait until we were given the instructions to fire, and it would be automatic because a clock would be set going on the bridge and that clock would give the signal to the stern rails to release the four charges. It would then give the instructions to the four beam stalks to fire, and again the final instructions for the rails to let go of their final four or six charges. It was automatic to that extent. Once we'd fire, it was reloaded and the pistols reset and the primers on the charges and again we waited until we'd come full circle and were going to make another attack. You could always tell, you had sufficient warning to be ready because once you'd turned away from your first attack you'd then come round, you'd then increase your speed as you went into the attack, so with all those feelings and noises, and you knew what was going to happen, so you got yourself ready; didn't really wait for instructions. You knew you were going to use them again. They were ready. The only thing that you would require would be a possible change in the setting on the pistols. The pistols themselves, how they worked, was that there was a graduated series of small holes set into the pistol, and when you pushed the key in and set it to one of the depths you would then have those holes that let in the water pressure. And once the water pressure had reached its level it would fire the pistol [against the detonator in] the primer which would explode the charge. (*Dykes*)

The first indication of a U-boat attack would be from the asdic people who would pick up a contact, and if they thought it was a submarine, or they could tell the difference between a submarine or a shoal of fish, they would immediately warn the officer of the watch, who would then sound action stations. Now that could go off any time of the day or night, so if you came off watch at twelve o'clock after having the first watch and just got turned in and about half-past twelve the rattlers went, as we called it, we were then to action stations. So the first thing they would do, the guns crew would line up, the depth-charge crew would line up and they'd report to the bridge, because they've got a little winding thing that they wind and it makes a buzzing noise up on the bridge and they'd say, 'Depth-charge rails closed up, port starboard rails closed up.' You know, 'Guns crews closed up, action station!' Well then the asdic rating would then be tracking the course of this contact that he had and you could hear the pings – ping, ping, ping, ping – and the difference between the ping and the pong is the distance how far the submarine is away. When they think they're right over the top of the submarine, the order is 'Fire!'. That means the depth-charges go. On our ship, I don't know about the other ships, but the first depth-charge would go off the stern and that would go off at about 50 feet, and it was almost as though you were lifted up in the air in the boat and dropped down again. A colossal volume of water would come up, and as the depth-charges were deeper (they were set with different depths), it was almost like lightning going across the water. In the daytime it's a fantastic thing to see. And then if you had a contact and you sunk the submarine you'd be waiting to see the telltale signs. Sometimes there'd be a false alarm. (*Stephens*)

I think it was the *Sunflower* that depth-charged a submarine and brought it to the surface, and we were within gun range of it, opened fire on it, and they tried to fire back, but they couldn't get to their gun because our gunfire was keeping them off. And then somebody on there waved a white flag, you see. We ceased fire and we were going alongside to pick up survivors and board the U-boat when we got another asdic reading, and we cleared off to chase this other U-boat. And as we just got out of range of the U-boat, she blew up. And had we gone alongside to pick up survivors we'd have gone up with her. She'd have taken us down too. But that was the nearest one I think we ever came to actually being sunk. (*Goldsmith*)

An extract from a 'Report of Proceedings from the Commander-in-Chief, Western Approaches, Admiral Percy Noble to HMS Campanula, *HMS* Honeysuckle *and HMS* Periwinkle *(Royal Naval Museum Collection)*

Our first ['Hedgehog'] effort with the U-boat was off Newfoundland and it proved a failure, because we came across the U-boat very quickly, action stations were sounded, but the impellers on these mortars were fitted with a cap which had three spring-loaded clips on it, so before you could start to fire the thing you had to take all these twenty-four caps off with these clips, and we were unable to get these caps off in time, so we had to abort the attack and start again. This had not been realized on the training ashore that it would take so long.

The gun we had on the ship was of Great War vintage, of course, like many of the ships, but still perfectly workable. And we did fire it very often because sometimes you had the U-boats coming in on the surface to attack a convoy. They were much faster on the surface than we were: our maximum speed was about 15 knots; they could do about 22 knots. So they could run away from us. So very often we would elevate the gun to its maximum and try and hit them on the horizon, not very successfully I'm afraid. And then sometimes we would fire a star shell at night to illuminate a submarine which we might have discovered by radar on the surface. (*Richmond*)

I remember on one occasion when I did fire an Oerlikon at a dive-bomber. I wasn't firing at the pilot; I was firing at the aircraft to try and damage it sufficient for it to hit the sea, and I think basically that's all

HMS Circassia, *Frank Richmond, 1940*
(courtesy Frank Richmond)

we were interested in. We didn't see the pilot. It wasn't a personal relationship between the chap sitting in the aircraft and myself. We couldn't see him. It was the plane we wanted to shoot down. And if we shot it down we would have picked the pilot up. (*Dykes*)

Most of the time at night I remember vessels being sunk in the centre of a convoy and you had to go and pick people up and you knew that the submarines were about. You'd get an echo, you dropped your depth-charge pad and sometimes they worked, sometimes they didn't. We didn't pick up any survivors in boats. *Anemone* did, at a later date, but I wasn't in on that one. But most of the time it was very boring, some of the time it was fairly frightening. And all the time it was very wet. (*Arthur*)

Escorts were fairly safe, you know they wouldn't normally waste a torpedo on a thing like a 'Flower' class corvette, unless it got in the way. There were a few accidents where they had been accidentally sunk and there'd been collisions between two corvettes, or a collision between a merchant ship and a corvette. That sort of general thing went on. I suppose the most dramatic [explosion] you would see was when you hear this almighty bang and you find the ship has split in two, and the bows were cocked up in the air and the stern was cocked up in the air, and both were sliding slowly back into the water. And that was quite a common sight really. (*Grant*)

There were tin hats on the gun platforms and we always wore life-jackets. One of the things that you see in a lot of pictures today is that [then] officers didn't wear life-jackets – they used to carry them round their shoulder. But ratings, or most of them, certainly anybody who was on convoy work, I think would have worn his lifebelt, which was really just like a motor cycle inner tube, with a stockinet thing over it. Very effective, they were very effective. I can remember coming back from one convoy, whereby we saw a body in the water still being supported by its lifebelt and it turned out to be one of the Norwegian sailors from the *Bath*, so he'd been in the water three weeks and that life-jacket, this rubber tyre thing, was still keeping him afloat. He was dead, yes.

We had a thing about clean overalls, and I think most people had two or three pairs of overalls, so you always had a clean pair of overalls, so you could sleep in your overalls which really wasn't much different to a pair of pyjamas. And if you did have to get out on the upper deck they were fairly windproof, that was one of the advantages of them. So I can't honestly say that I was caught unawares. (*Drummond*)

You never knew what the hell was going on. I've had to read books about it since to find out what was going on. I don't think anybody knows. You do what you're told to do, and you don't know what. You don't know if you've got a submarine, because you very seldom see any effect of what you're doing; it may come up much later when you've come out of the area. (*Arthur*)

'Brave Professionals'

THE MERCHANT SEAMEN

In the main, they themselves were unprotected by their
own armament, had to rely on others for protection, and
I think that, bearing in mind the cargoes they carried at
times, they were very, very brave professionals.

HOLLINSHED

Well, I think we were all going through the same sort of thing. We were in the same sort of danger, although probably we didn't recognize it as

HMS Anemone, *survivors from HX229 on board, Atlantic, 1943* (courtesy Edgar Pomeroy)

danger at that time, but you were in it together. There was no running
away from it, was there? You were there and you had to get on with it.
(*Drummond*)

I personally felt that they [the Merchant seamen] had a harder life than we
had, through anxiety. We were moving around; we could zig-zag; we could
do anything we liked. If I didn't know what zig-zag I was going to do,
then no one else would. But you get a merchant ship, [which] had to steer
a course, stay in the same position, keep his speed up, because if he let his
speed go then he was going to be on his own and he's going to have
possibly seven days or longer on his own in the ocean and he didn't stand
much of a chance to complete his trip. And even when they were under
attack [there was] nothing that they could do. They couldn't alter course.
They still had to carry on with their course, continue their course and their
speed. Hopefully they wouldn't be the next one to be attacked. I well
remember seeing in the daylight in the convoy a merchant ship. There
were two torpedoes on the surface, breaking the surface. You could see
them running on the surface, and there was this merchant ship and on the
upper deck, on the boat deck was this man pointing out these two
torpedoes as they came in. Now, where we were, you couldn't really see
whether they were going to hit that ship or not, but they did. They hit the

Survivors from the Richmond Castle, *picked up by HMS* Snowflake, *1942 (courtesy Howard Goldsmith)*

ship amidships and within a matter of seconds there was nothing left, no survivors or anything. But they couldn't take avoiding action because they couldn't, no merchant ship, in those days, could alter course quick enough to avoid it. I think that they really were sitting ducks and they must have had tension, great concern, great worry. (*Dykes*)

I think one's got to give and admire tremendously the courage of the merchant seamen because they were really like sitting ducks. They were sailing in a constant direction, at a constant speed, and they really had only the Navy to protect them. So I think a lot of the credit . . . they deserve a lot of admiration those people, a lot of admiration. I mean some of them did manage to sink U-boats, of course. Many of them had guns on their fo'c's'le and many of them had depth-charges. (*Richmond*)

We had great respect for the Merchant seamen. I think they were underestimated, especially now by the British public today, because they talk about the Battle of Britain. Granted the pilots did a marvellous, marvellous job, but when you stop and think, how did they get the fuel across to fly those planes, it was the Merchant seamen. And if you've ever seen a tanker go up in flames, my golly! You hear this terrific roar and this one great sheet of flame and then there's nothing, just like that. And, honestly, I think they're

Survivors from Nariva *and* Canadian Star *on board HMS* Anemone, *1943*
(courtesy Edgar Pomeroy)

the bravest men out, the Merchant Navy, The corvette boys had a great respect for the man in the Merchant Navy and likewise the Merchant Navy had for us, because they used to say, 'We don't know how you fellows live aboard them things, because sometimes we see a bit of a funnel and then we don't see anything for a while, then we see a bit more funnel.' (*Stephens*)

[When] Merchant ships were torpedoed, rescues were being made, usually by the escorts, but quite often the Merchantmen did some of the rescuing themselves. (*Drummond*)

'The Pitiful State of People'
SURVIVORS

But the pitiful state of people that you have to try to handle into a boat, you know, when everything is slipping through your grasp. I mean nothing could be retained after its been contaminated by oil fuel. It's thick oil fuel; it clings to everything. I mean, it must be the most awful thing for survivors.

DRUMMOND

I think probably the things that stand out in my memory more than anything are the cries of people amongst the wreckage after a ship had been torpedoed. The hustle and bustle of climbing into a boat, being lowered, getting it all away, and then, while your own ship may well be some distance away, listening to what might be called 'the quiet of the sea', but then the human voices coming into the picture. Where are they? What is the distance? Because in those days quite a number of people didn't have lights on their life-jackets, and quite a number of people that you picked up didn't have life-jackets at all. And so the human cries, the pitiful sort of appearance of the people in the water, getting them into your own boat and then trying to get back to your own ship as quickly as you could, to unload that lot and get off for another load. Well, I think those are the things that probably stay in my memory, quite vividly to this day. (*Drummond*)

The corvettes didn't have any what you'd call watertight arrangements, like they've got now, watertight compartments. They were quite open. The bunk space was a big, wide-open space. The mess-deck was, the boiler room was, the engine room was and there wasn't much left after that. And they were quite big compartments and the ship's side was very, very thin steel. There was no armour-plating or anything like that. So you could say that, if they got a torpedo or a mine, then the chances of the ship remaining afloat were very, very remote and the chances of all the men surviving were also very remote – generally speaking. (*Grant*)

mae

A lot of the chaps didn't wear their 'May Wests', you know their lifebelts, and were non-swimmers, and I think a lot of those were lost. (*James*)

And quite often, there'd been occasions when you heard cries for help, but you couldn't get round to them quick enough. I mean, our ship's lifeboat was 16 foot long, not a very big boat [about the size of a Wayfarer sailing dinghy, so they were not very big for the job they were called upon to do]. And there have been a couple of occasions when I had to leave two of my crew behind, and just take the lifeboat with two people in so's you could get more people in. But the thing that always went through your mind was some people who cried out for help, by the time you got to them, [they] weren't there any longer. And I think that that's something that sticks a bit with you, even to this day. (*Drummond*)

There was the time when we were bringing a convoy from Halifax. We were getting quite hard pressed because we were always aware at the early evening, about five o'clock, six o'clock, of the number of U-boats in contact with the convoy, and it would have been about seven or eight o'clock at night when this convoy was attacked. It was a very dark night, very black, couldn't see the horizon or anything. [The convoy] was attacked and the ship, USS *Pink Star*, was torpedoed, and we lowered the dinghy to pick up survivors and we took a long time picking them up, because there were quite a number of survivors to rescue. Eventually the ship sank, and as it sank the fires went out, so we were completely in the dark, and by then also the small personal red lights which each seaman carried on his shoulder would have gone out, either because the batteries had gone out or the water would have destroyed them. We eventually came across a man who earlier had been singing – singing hymns if I remember rightly – [whilst his ship was on fire, the sea also on fire and he clinging to a lifeboat alongside the stricken ship]. We found him quite by accident. He was just floating with his life-jacket covered in oil and he was pretty well unconscious by the time we found him.

It had been about 25 minutes or so after the ship had sunk, and he was so heavy that we couldn't get him on board over the side of the dinghy, so we had to take him astern, take the rudder and tiller out of the dinghy and bring him over the stern and [into the dinghy]. In fact he had two lifebelts on. He was pretty well unconscious; he was in a terrible state. He had one leg that

OPPOSITE AND ABOVE: *Torpedoed British Merchant seamen rescued by HMS* Snowflake, *1942* *(courtesy George Ambler)*

was very hard, as if it had been frozen, and it was remarked that, 'Well if he's frozen, let's throw him back over the side again.' Anyhow, we kept him, and he laid in the bottom of the dinghy and [eventually] we got him on board and he turned out to be alright. It also proved that this very hard leg was an artificial leg, so his two life-jackets basically were to keep him afloat. He couldn't have kept afloat with one leg. He was an elderly man, getting on for his late sixties, if not into the seventies. A retired American master mariner, he had come back into the American Merchant Navy to help this country – 'the old lady', as he called her – and inside his artificial leg were rolls upon rolls of American dollars, which basically was all his worldly goods, which we dried out for him in the boiler room, and handed them back to him when we returned to Liverpool. (*Dykes*)

The Atlantic is extremely cold, even in the best times of the year, in the summer. And chances of surviving in the water for any length of time were fairly remote. And then the other terrible hazard was, of course, if a tanker was hit and oil spilled out onto the surface of the sea. Then anybody who

An extract from a diary of RDF operator Donald Canham (*courtesy Helen Canham*)

survived usually had taken in oil into their mouth, their stomach. [They] were covered in oil and many of them didn't survive through that. And it's very difficult to pick up survivors. I mean, we used to have scrambling nets [over the side], but when they're covered in oil it's very difficult to get to grips with them. And sometimes, unfortunately, you could only stay for a limited time to pick up survivors, because our prime duty was, as I say, to protect the convoy. That's why, eventually, we had rescue ships detailed, which were small merchant ships, which were detailed off to run at the rear of the convoy and pick up survivors.

Generally speaking it was those seamen who were on deck who survived. On oil tankers there was very, very few who survived, of course. But generally it was the people on deck who had a chance. And if they could be picked up fairly quickly there was a good chance they would live. (*Richmond*)

Some rescues were made by one of us putting a heaving line round ourselves and swimming out. Particularly if survivors were in their own boat, hanging onto the lifeboat and then getting pulled in. Saved a lot of time. You could get people in quicker that way. But, of course, where survivors were individuals in the sea you needed to lower your own boat. (*Drummond*)

I don't know whether any did survive, there was about twenty, but if any survived I don't know. But they were all in the same situation. Oil – you should see the oil coming out of their mouths every time they coughed. It was a real state, black. They were black but they were absolutely covered in oil. And burned patches on them, burned hair off. Awful! Not a very nice sight. (*Taylor*)

I remember one occasion when early in the morning about five, we were behind the convoy rescue vessel and a ship had been torpedoed. And we were picking up some survivors, and we came across a raft in daylight, and there were two men on it. And when we came alongside they said, 'There are some people further astern', and pointed down, you see, so we left them on the raft. They said, 'Go on, go on, go.' Very noble of them. And we went about 5 miles; couldn't find these people; they were drowned obviously, and when we came back we couldn't find the raft. And, of course, I had to send a man up to the crow's nest – it was rolling like the son of a gun – to finally spot them. They were still there, by the grace of God, and we got them. (*Atkinson*)

Some of the time in convoys when the ships were hit you'd try and fish people out of the water. In the dark it's a fairly unpleasant business. When you slowed down you felt that everybody is watching you through a periscope and you weren't quite sure when you saw something bobbing in the water whether it was a Cheshire cheese or a man's head. (*Arthur*)

And all around, because a number of ships were going down. And all around for as far as you could see, there were little lights and voices calling out, 'Here I am. Here I am.' But you could do little. You couldn't pick 'em up; you couldn't stop; you couldn't pick 'em up. And so that was it, and maybe some of them were looking next morning, but no way could we pick 'em up at night at all, although we saw all these red lights. We knew what they were. [They were the little red lights they had on their life-jackets]. They came on automatic, so you hit the water you pull a little cord and they used to come on. And you see 'em dotted all over the place, but you couldn't do anything about it. (*Hallam*)

We used to put special nets over the side, big 8-inch squares, and just drop them over the side, and hang them on the side so a man could grasp them, you see. And many times if a ship was torpedoed, especially tankers, the

Atlantic lifesaver – a safety lamp (*Royal Naval Museum Collection*)

ocean would be thick with oil and they would die quickly. And one had to make choices. You sometimes saw two or three men swimming, and you would say go for them and leave him, because he was on his own. Well, that meant that he would drown, but it was impersonal. You never saw that poor man, you'd hear him calling but you couldn't pick 'em all up, and furthermore it was quite dangerous to stop and pick up men, in as much as if a ship had been torpedoed, that meant that a submarine was there, so he would know you were stopping. He might just line you up and torpedo you, so if you stopped you had to do it suddenly and without warning, and you had to be quite skilled at that as well. (*Atkinson*)

I remember one night we cleared as much of the corvette as we possibly could and took all these poor Merchant seamen on, most of them black. They were all Lascars [Indians] I think, mainly Lascars. And we took them on board. They were full of oil; they were burned; they'd been swimming in a flaming sea, and we took them on board. And we had to lay them all the way down from one end of the ship to the other, where we could, in all the passages that we could. We only had one medic on board, a French sick-berth attendant. So anyone who knew anything about first aid gave a hand, and he had to use a limited supply of medicines. He did a very good job. Unfortunately, most of them died, by coughing up oil, and he said, I remember him saying, 'Well, we're not going to have many of these left at the end of the day.' And there was no one that we could transfer them to, as we were in a situation in the convoy at that moment where we just couldn't stop. We daren't stop and transfer people over, just had to carry on. If you'd stopped, you'd have been tin-fished right away, no doubt about that. (*Taylor*)

Well, quite a number of survivors had broken limbs. They had either broken arms or legs. One or two would have quite severe internal injuries, and I did

The ship's boat of HMS Hesperus, *mid-Atlantic, 1943* (*courtesy Frank Richmond*)

have one or two who died while they were in the boat, you know, being transferred. And they would subsequently have to be buried at sea. But I suppose the worst thing probably was the oil fuel. The difficulty, perhaps, from a survivor's point of view was that quite often you were handling people, trying to hoist them into the boat and you didn't realize that they had broken arms or broken legs. They would scream then, would the survivors. But, of course, you weren't to know that, you were away in a boat, your aim was to get them in the boat and get them back to the ship to some safety. (*Drummond*)

Just to clean them up was a problem. But to try and expel this oil that was inside them was awful, because it went into their lungs and everywhere, plus water of course. Some, of course, would be very badly burned by the explosion, or by the oil catching alight or petrol catching alight. That often happened. (*Richmond*)

Some survivors you picked up weren't covered in oil fuel. Some had had a pretty clean run. But for those that were, we eventually started to carry benzene, which you could get the thick of it all off with, but most of the time the first-aid parties you might say, or anybody, that could be anybody,

Survivors from Canadian Star, *picked up by HMS* Anemone, *1943. Left to right: Colonel L.P. Crouch, Mrs Dobree and Mr Dobree (courtesy George Ambler)*

because we carried no doctor, would be getting him on his side trying to get him to cough and vomit. Sometimes I think there was a record of one survivor being asked to take a few puffs of a cigarette, and he was protesting quite strongly to say that he didn't smoke, but the idea was by making him smoke, to make him cough and bring up this sort of mass of oil fuel that he'd swallowed. So there wasn't a great deal that you could do with them. The main thing was to try and get it out of their eyes, as much as you could, and then provide for them. In the early stages of the war by clothing from all our blokes. You know, you chucked in clothing to help him out. But later on, probably 1942 time, we started to carry survivors kits, which was a great help really. [They had] a complete change of underwear, and a type of overall suit that they could put on – a woolly pully, obviously donated by the Red Cross or the WRVS, people like that, or towns that had adopted ships. So that was quite good. Some shoe wear, usually in the form of gym shoes, that sort of thing. Towels, toothpaste, you know, basic sort of things that people wanted. (*Drummond*)

Being a boarding officer, or seaboat officer, really, it was my responsibility to take the dinghy away and pick up as many survivors as we could possibly carry, and take them back to the ship and then go back again if there were more survivors. They usually were in a very distressed state, as you can imagine. Even just a man that possibly jumped over the ship before it sank and we picked him up immediately. The traumatic experience for him having to get up onto the upper deck on his own ship and then getting out as quick as he could was sufficient an experience to give him a lot of shock. But then, of course, there were others who had been burned by fire, or covered in oil, and also had got it in their lungs and were in a very bad state. And also hypothermia, as we know it today, could have set in by the time we picked them up. Just rowing around in the Atlantic is not an easy matter, particularly if there's a swell. They might be on rafts, or hanging to something or just swimming in their own life-jacket. It didn't help them whatsoever. When they got on board, we would clean them up as much as it was possible to do so. The injuries would be seen by an officer and also the sick-berth attendant, and we would give them dry clothing. We did receive, or we did have on board, what were known as survivor kits, which would have a change of clothing for them, dry clothing and Horlicks tablets, to give them a bit of strength, a packet of cigarettes, that sort of thing, just to give them some degree of comfort after such an experience. (*Dykes*)

We had no doctor on board. We had what was called a sick-berth attendant. And he would be given every help to clean the guys up and to reclothe them and look after them generally. Some, of course, unfortunately, didn't survive. The standard practice [then] was to sew them up in canvas sheeting and to weight them at the feet end, and then the captain would slow the ship down. He would go down to the stern; he would read a prayer out of the bible and the ship would slow down, the board would be tipped, it would be covered with a White Ensign and the White Ensign would be held onto with the board and the body would just slip down into the water. (*Richmond*)

The look-out spotted a boat on the horizon, or an object on the horizon, which turned out to be a ship's boat, with about fifteen men in it. And we got them aboard. Some of them were in a pretty bad

A survivor from Canadian Star, *cleaning her coat on HMS* Anemone, *1943 (courtesy Edgar Pomeroy)*

way, and they were the survivors of the *Richmond Castle*, which had been sunk by a German U-boat and had been adrift for about fourteen days – fourteen, fifteen days. One had pleurisy, one had very severe wounds to his legs, which had gone more or less gangrenous, and there were other injuries and illnesses amongst them. And it was a bit like painting the Eiffel Tower, because I was treating them and then having about 10 minutes break and then back to the first one again and round to the others. I did that for about five days, until we got back to harbour. I'm very pleased to say that they all survived – at least they were all alive when they left the ship. And most of them were very much improved in health. They were a lot better. (*Goldsmith*)

What I did notice was quite a lot of survivors, once you'd got them on board and got them cleaned up, weren't very keen on sleeping below decks. They would tend to find places around the funnel, where it was a bit warmer, engine-room casings, that sort of thing. They weren't too keen at that particular stage to stay down below decks. I'm sure it stays with them for the rest of their lives. I don't think they ever get over it. (*Drummond*)

Survivors from Canadian Star, *picked up by* HMS Anemone, *1943. Wing Commander Wrigley and his daughter Maureen. Mrs Wrigley's back was broken during the rescue and she was buried at sea* (courtesy Edgar Pomeroy)

No, most of these chaps had still got traces of oil on them, but they'd been so long – fourteen days – they'd got most of it off themselves. But I picked up the results of the oil in the form of the infected wounds damaged by the oil and, of course, skin problems, burns, oil burns and that sort of thing. There wasn't much you could do in those days. Calamine was probably the standby. If they were still covered in oil we used an oil to get it off – cooking oil, butter whatever you had handy to clean it off. The medical advances in the last fifty years, people don't realize how comparatively primitive medicine was in those days. The drugs weren't there; they weren't available. And you had to use things that now you'd think twice about. I mean, we used an awful lot of salt, common salt, in the form of a normal saline. Wonderful stuff, it heals, it's an antiseptic, can't do any harm, but it just takes a little longer; it takes longer than the modern drugs do. But we hadn't got them. We hadn't got those things, you see. (*Goldsmith*)

There was another incident where we picked up a survivor and he was on his own, and he was on a raft. And we picked him up just before we were due to get into Newfoundland. And he had been on the raft for about ten days. I think he told us that originally there were about five on the raft, but they'd all died one by one. But after he'd been on board for a couple of days, we found that he had a bit of a psychiatric problem which had obviously been affected by [his experience], and he would bash his head against the sides of the ship, and would get hold of your arm and say, 'I'd like to eat your arm', things like that. So eventually we had to have him locked up, and when we got into St John's they came and took him away. But he'd obviously been affected by his experiences on this raft. (*Grant*)

Space was at a premium, of course. Standing room only perhaps would be a better term in some of the cases. But the wardroom was used, as were our bunks, in all those cases of injury. But many convoys [later] had a rescue ship which had all first-aid facilities, medical facilities, and when possible [the survivors] were transferred to the rescue ship. They were looked after, so that although we only had supplies for our own ship's company, and these people exhausted our supplies to some extent, we were not eaten out of house and home. (*Hollinshed*)

The clothing kit? It was to replace damaged clothing. Some people you picked up were virtually naked. They would want clothing. Well, our chaps carried their own sort of clothing, but once you'd done a few trips with survivors, you were running short on your own particular clothing. Food wise, I mean, I don't think any survivor would have ever gone short. Rations would have been shared in the same sort of way as it ever was. I think on one occasion [survivors] were taken on board, and I think there was somewhere in the region of 300 and odd people. Well, of course, if you get numbers like that on to a corvette, it's not going to be very long before you've got no food at all. But fortunately they sent a team of their own crew back to their ship and she was taken under tow, but then they got her own engines to work so the crew could go back on board. So that relieved us. I think we scrounged some stores off them in the end because she was an AMC, you see, an armed Merchant cruiser. (*Drummond*)

The injured would be put into a bunk. We'd give up our accommodation to them. But the uninjured, even those that had got covered in oil or just the traumatic experience of being a survivor, they would just sit on the mess-decks. They would most likely, in the end, play cards or something like that, just to pass the time away. (*Dykes*)

In May, I think it was '41, we had a signal come through to go out to meet [a ship that had] been escorting an Italian tanker home and they had a bit of trouble on board the Italian tanker, so they stopped and were going to put more crew aboard her and a submarine came up and sunk both of them. And I remember it was the *Heather* came with us to try and find these survivors, and a stoker came off watch, about just after four o'clock, and he was leant on the rails and he said, 'What's that over there?' And it was a fellow in a boat waving an oar, and we went alongside them and we picked up 126 survivors and we took them into the Clyde. They came down into the mess-decks, and we fed and clothed them best we could and gave up our bunks for them. Compared to some corvettes – some corvettes had a terrific amount of survivors on them, 200 sometimes. And when you consider that the crew of a corvette was about fifty, you can tell what the poor old cook in the galley had to contend with. You've always got the tins of baked beans and sausages and all that type of stuff, but as regards bread and fresh meat, that'd gone long ago. (*Stephens*)

Perhaps my greatest experience with survival was with HMS *Pink*. Early one morning a Liberator was being . . . we could see him being shot at by a submarine over the horizon, and he was on fire and I could see him on fire flying around. And I [signalled] 'Ditch beside me, K137', and he came flying around and ditched beside me. He thought it was calm because he couldn't quite see from high up, but, of course, it wasn't calm and he hit the ocean and did about two somersaults and dived straight in. That crew was so well trained. We had one man on board in less than 1 minute and two of them were dead. We buried them at sea with a proper service. One had a compound fracture of the leg, which we had to bind. We had no doctor and we just pressed on to Newfoundland, and we were separated from the convoy and I picked up three stragglers and took them along with me. And I think we [also] sank a submarine that time. But, of course, the man was ill, and we asked to enter the harbour and [were told], 'The harbour's closed after dark, but we will open the gates for you at midnight and for 15 minutes after the hour, every hour for three hours only.' And we didn't quite know where we were because there was dense fog, cold, icebergs. So we cut south about 20 miles and went straight inshore. And I put about twenty people on the

*HMS Pink, rescuing the crew of a Liberator shot down by a U-boat in mid-Atlantic,
15 October 1942 (from the collection of Dr and Mrs Brian Swinscoe, courtesy the artist, Terry
Rogers, ex-HMS Bergamot)*

look-out that night and said, 'The first thing you'll see are the cliffs. If you
see them, you'll be 100 feet from them, and we'll be edging in slowly. The
first person who hears anything, shout like hell.' Well, I was never very good
at hearing, but I was the best that night. And I heard the whooo! whooo! [of
the fog horns]. Newfoundland. We went on at great speed. They'd put all the
lights on for us and we took those men into harbour and got the ambulances
within a few minutes. They were waiting for us alongside and whipped them
all away. (*Atkinson*)

CHAPTER FOUR

CONDITIONS ON BOARD

Very wet. At times the amount of water coming over the fo'c's'le meant that water was finding its way into the mess-decks. But the crews, I think, did an enormous job in keeping their living quarters clean.

Montague 'John' Hollinshed, RNVR, 1938–1946;
Watchkeeping Officer, HMS HEATHER

Conditions on board a corvette were quite stark. Accommodation for the officers was in small, cramped cabins. For the ratings it was on overcrowded mess-decks where men packed in tightly together, some even sleeping on mess-top tables. The cramped accommodation was eased slightly when the corvettes were modified and the fo'c's'les were extended. The atmosphere down below, however, changed little. There was negligible ventilation, little light and the air was murky with the smell of smoke, wet clothes, sweat and vomit. Food was basic. Fresh meat and vegetables were soon consumed and then it depended on the ingenuity of the cook as to how appetizing tinned food and hard biscuits could be. Kye, slab cocoa and the customary tot, however, were perennial sources of solace. Washing and sanitary facilities were equally basic. The officers had a small washbasin in their cabins, but the ratings made do with a galvanized bucket. The heads were similarly primitive, doors flapping open to the elements. Clothing, including overalls, which were worn, for the most part, day and night, and duffle-coats and sou'westers, was mostly warm. A constant problem, however, was the wet, and all struggled, often in vain, to keep the water from dripping down their necks.

'A Hammock to Sling'
GENERAL ACCOMMODATION

I was in the seamen's for'ard mess-deck because I was a leading seaman at that particular time, and I had a bunk, which was a bit of a luxury to me, really, as it was right for'ard in the ship. It seemed alright while you were in harbour, but when you got to sea it was a different story. So at least I didn't have a hammock to sling. Some people did have to sling hammocks, 'cos there weren't bunks for everybody.

DRUMMOND

[Conditions were wet] especially when you had the short fo'c's'le, because in a heavy sea she'd dip about twice and the third time look out, because it'd come over in tons of water, and if you happened to be outside, there was no way you could stand up to that pressure; you were probably washed down the deck. (*Stephens*)

Your first problem was to get out of the mess-deck. Unbolt, take the hatches off and get out of the mess-deck and into the well-deck. And then you had to grope your way along to a position near the funnel, where you had to climb up and over the top of the boiler and get down that way [to get out]. Because you couldn't go down the escape hatch; you couldn't open it, because you'd 'ave shipped a load of water in there and that would have been it. So if you had to go to the engine room, worse still, because you had that same distance to go again on the upper deck. You've no passages to walk through; it was all open, the whole deck was open, from the bridge to the fo'c's'le. (*Hallam*)

I think they were very hard physical conditions. Inside was dampness too, in the mess-decks, trying to keep the steam heating [working] to keep them warm. And I think those are the conditions that would easily lead to TB. As a matter of fact, the only time I've ever been ill in my life was after that. I came home, and I was not well for a month. And I left the *Pink* and went to *Tintagel Castle*, but it was the severity of that arctic winter – the seasickness, the exposure, the anxiety, the poor food, etcetera. One doesn't realize this. We're all young, we're all strong – or think we are, or hope we are – but a doctor will tell you after a month or two months of those conditions, anybody begins to decline. But the crew were marvellous; stood up to it. (*Atkinson*)

Since the fo'c's'le had been extended, the accommodation, of course, was larger in that there was more accommodation in passageways, which eased the crush in the mess-deck proper. (*Hollinshed*)

Now when I joined *Anemone* she had a short fo'c's'le with a well-deck for'ard and the mast was for'ard of the bridge, which meant that you were in terrible isolation. You had to cross the well-deck to get into the shelter of the mess-deck. And then you were allocated. 'This is where you're going to sling your hammock.' And, of course, that's where you slung your hammock. I remember the very first night, I slung my hammock and I was a bit tired or emotional or something and, when rounds – there's always rounds at night when the officer of the watch comes round and inspects everything to see they're okay – and somebody very kindly let down my hammock, with me inside it, as he arrived. (*Arthur*)

One of the worst things I found there [on HMS *Campanula*] was the well-deck. To go from for'ard, which all the ship's company were, all underneath the fo'c's'le, all for'ard, nobody aft at all, only petty officers. And if you wanted to get from your mess-deck to the galley you took your life in your hands. The galley was right aft [with an open well-deck], and as you opened the door sometimes the bulkhead door from the mess-deck, if you shipped a big wave, it followed you into the mess-deck and, of course, everybody wore

HMS Snowflake, *the crew catch a few winks, Atlantic, 1943* (courtesy Cyril Hatton)

sea boots. It was a very tricky job. Very dangerous, I should say, to go from for'ard to aft, until they modified them and they enclosed all that, what we call the well-deck, made it comparatively safe then to get from for'ard to aft. But when you go from for'ard in action stations, on a nasty night and that, onto an open-deck, it's not very clever. (*Hallam*)

So far as the watch-keeping officer was concerned, we slept two to a cabin, apart from the first lieutenant who was on his own, and the skipper who, of course, had his own cabin. But the mess-decks were very, very difficult. Accommodation was very, very limited. The ship's company slept on mess-top tables, locker-top tables, the deck, in fact they slept anywhere which was reasonably dry. Hammocks were rarely slung since there was very little room for hammocks. (*Hollinshed*)

[A corvette] had cabins that were situated on what was called the wardroom flat, which was the deck about level with the water line. A small wardroom, some 15 foot by 15 foot square, leading into a wardroom flat. And from that there were three cabins, one first lieutenant and two subs. That basically was the accommodation in those days. Of course, that improved when they extended the fo'c's'le deck above the funnel, the result of that being they had more accommodation for officers on what was then the upper deck. So because of that we had two more officers appointed and, on the whole, they were comfortable ships. (*Dykes*)

It wasn't sleeping accommodation as such. The mess-deck had a long covered mess table and benches beside it. And you had hammock netting. Now, when you got out of your hammock, you were supposed to lash up and stow, which meant that you had to put on seven turns on the hammock, one for each day of the week, and put in the hammock netting. Hammock netting is an old Nelson term, because the hammocks used to be put on the side of the vessel to stop the shot coming through. So in daytime the mess-deck was clear of hammocks. But at night it was totally covered with a layer of about 4 foot off the ground, so you had to sort of crawl underneath these sleeping bodies. But a hammock is great to sleep in because you curl in. You have your bed, which is a sort of flock-filled little tiny mattress and your blanket, and there you curl up and every time the ship pitches and rolls the hammock takes a lot of the sway out. So you really are very comfortable and snug. (*Arthur*)

You used to hop out of bed, whenever you went on duty, and onto the mess table. And if there was anything left on the mess table, you put your foot in

HMS Snowflake, *the crew resting off Iceland, 1943* (courtesy Cyril Hatton)

it, you know. And, of course, the scuttles were always closed, so you couldn't get any fresh air except when we were in the harbour. And it really is a wonder that we didn't all get TB or something like that, I should think. Because it really smelt down there, especially when you'd been on watch for four hours in a howling gale, and you came down below. You fought yourself down there into the murk, and, as I say, I think we handled it better than the older people. I felt quite sorry for them, as sorry as I could be at my age. (*Donkin*)

You had hammocks – most of the ship had hammocks. There were [a limited number of] bunks. As different people left the ship they had a rota, and you could move up to get a bunk. I had one when I left – well I'd been on [board] for about six months. And I qualified for this bunk and it was alright, but I didn't mind the hammock. It was pretty good if you rig it right. The only trouble, there wasn't enough room on a corvette for the hammocks. Sometimes you stepped on the mess table, sometimes on a stool. If there was a stanchion, you might get three hammocks in a line, or on two stanchions. And, funny thing, no matter how drunk blokes got, they could always get in their hammock. They could always seem to swing up and get in their hammock – strange really. Getting out was harder, but getting in, they always seemed to make it. (*Jolly*)

There were hammocks and bunks. We had a bunk. There was probably about twenty down the lower bunk space, twenty in our sleeping quarters down below. And there were bunks on the mess-deck and hammock slinging billets. Phew! Why we never finished up with TB, heaven only knows. Because when you went off watch and went down below, the stench was awful; it was like a sewer. Because you had probably wet washing, wet clothes on steam pipes trying to dry, you had water floating around all over the place, people being sick, you know, sweaty socks. It was awful, it really was, it was awful. (*Stephens*)

The bunks used to drop down on chains from the ship's side, although they were never put back up again. You'd come off watch and you'd flop down, and that was it. (*Hallam*)

The worst part, I suppose, was that, when you were at sea in rough weather, [the corvettes] were thrown about like corks, and water was usually slushing about, not only in the bunk space but in the mess-decks as well, and because you were battened down the air was quite foul at the time. Of course, being a young man at the time – I was only nineteen – it didn't worry me all that much, but I think it must have affected the older men. If you was over about twenty-eight, we used to call them older men then. And some of them had wives and children, of course. They'd been called up from civilian life. At the time it didn't worry me, but in hindsight I now realize how much those chaps must have suffered, mentally and being so uncomfortable, too. (*Grant*)

Ventilation wasn't at it's best – certainly wasn't as good as the cruiser that I'd left, [where] we had forced ventilation pumped through the ship. Corvettes didn't have anything like that. They relied more on upper-deck ventilators, which if you turned them in the right direction you would get the force of the wind to push the air down below. If you bear in mind that when you went

Donald Canham when he first joined the Royal Navy, May 1941 (courtesy Helen Canham)

to sea everything was battened down, all the portholes were battened down with dead lights to prevent any light from getting out. Most of the ventilation units were turned aft so's that they wouldn't get too much of the seas inboard, so it got a bit stinky down below. If you were on the lower mess-deck, which invariably the stokers were, down there, quite often that would be awash with the water that had leaked through some of the seams. After you'd left the dockyard there was always something that was open, or that had leaked through ventilators or hatches. So it was a pretty damp sort of atmosphere. The other thing, I suppose, probably, that we suffered from more than anything was condensation. With all the body heat, you might say, with metal surrounding, you had this constant drip from deck heads into clothing . . . everything was always damp. (*Drummond*)

You had ventilation coming up through shafts, where they had to blow through and they had louvres on where you could regulate which way the air was going. But when we got in, obviously you rigged up the old air vents then. (*Stephens*)

The atmosphere downstairs was always 'fuggy', as they used to call it. In those days you smoked, of course, everybody smoked. In fact, you were encouraged to smoke during the war really. And because all portholes were closed up at sea, of course, ventilation was very poor. So the atmosphere could be quite thick at times. (*Richmond*)

If it was calm weather, which it very rarely was, you had what you called wind scoops which you push out the side, through the porthole, which caught the wind as the ship went along, which brought fresh air into the ship. But outside of that . . . there was fans, but again these weren't always working because the inlets were on the upper deck and these often had to be closed as well, and, of course, when that happened, the fans had to be switched off. We used to get plenty of fresh air really because we used to do four hours on and eight hours off. Well, the four hours on you was on the upper deck all the time – you really got enough fresh air to last you the next eight hours. (*Grant*)

[The lighting] was electric. You know, a pair of generators from the engine room. We had secondary lighting as well, little tiny blue lights, at night. (*Stephens*)

There were no lights on the upper deck but down below all lights were red, so you lived in rather a weird situation. But you got used to these red lights.

You could read; you could write. But the advantage was when you rushed up top into the pitch darkness, you could see very clearly where you were. You didn't stumble over things. You didn't hit each other or collide with each other, and it was a great asset to get acclimatized to the darkness quickly. (*Dykes*)

The pay was ludicrous. When I first joined up in 1942 it was 2s. a day. I don't think it was much more when I was an AB. And you didn't have much chance of spending it. You didn't need it for travel; you had all your travel warrants and so on. When you went ashore you could spend it if you wanted to on ice-cream or beer, or whatever you fancied. But three weeks at sea and nothing to spend it on, you had a bit of money when you went ashore. (*Arthur*)

We had a sick-berth attendant [but not till later on]. When we first commissioned, the coxswain used to do that job. But later on they allocated us a sick-berth attendant. I think that came about when the fo'c's'le was extended, because he had a little tiny cabin where he used to dole his stuff out. (*Stephens*)

Did we have a doctor? No we didn't. One case we had where a man was ill, he had a temperature, dreadful weather, couldn't quite understand what was wrong with him, but he was certainly getting worse. And I thought, in fact one of the men said to me he thought, it could be appendicitis, and it was obviously getting worse and we communicated with the escort commander, and, of course, the weather was too bad, and he said we might have to transfer the man to him. It was almost impossible to lower a boat, so we kept him on board for another day, and finally he really was bad and it was quite clear he had appendicitis. We thought peritonitis might develop and so we said to this man we're going to transfer you and he said no he didn't want to be transferred; he was frightened of the boat. It was so bad. And when you lower a boat like that, you can't just lower it into the sea. You have to wait for a moment and then you release [the slip] and the boat suddenly drops, so if you drop from 4 or 5 feet you're in trouble. You've got to wait till it's just touching the water. That requires skill. And the man refused to go. He said he won't go. So, as captain of the ship, I went along to see this man and sometimes how brutal life is, you have to be, and I said to this man, 'You're dying,' which gave him a great shock. And I said, 'You're going to die and there's nothing we can do about it, and we will have to bury you at sea.' And that really concentrated his mind, and he was extremely nervous, as he would be, and the man had a very high temperature. I said, 'The only thing we can do is to transfer you to the parent ship where there's a doctor on board, and if it is what I think it is, and the doctor thinks it might be from what I'm telling him, you might save your life. Otherwise there's no way you're going to live.' 'Alright.' He was so ill. We had to strap him to a board, the stretcher, and strap him in the boat. You couldn't lower the boat and put him into the boat. We had to put him into the boat before it was lowered, and he couldn't be moved, so he was rigid in that boat with the crew and it was dark. We waited till first light, and we dropped him and he was taken on board the ship and he had appendicitis, and they operated and it was successful and I was very gratified. (*Atkinson*)

'Cooks to the Galley'
MESSING

When there was the pipe, which usually went as I remember, 'Up-spirits, cooks to the galley', and 'cooks to the galley' meant those people who'd been designated cooks got the food from the galley. Now in the corvette with a short fo'c's'le, it meant that you had to go from the galley, which was on the quarter-deck, right aft, and you had to climb up a ladder with these great trays of food, go along the upper deck, and, when you got to the bridge, then you had to judge your thing right. You went down a ladder and you waited until the corvette had dipped it's nose, taken the sea on board, the sea had come sweeping over the well-deck, then you'd rush forward before it happened again, to get in in the dry. Otherwise you lost the food and got rather wet. It was quite exciting. When they made a longer fo'c's'le, then we didn't have that same problem.

ARTHUR

You didn't know how long the convoy was going to take. You see sometimes we could go across the Atlantic in about nine days and another time it would be about thirteen or fourteen days. All depends where the U-boat packs were. (*Stephens*)

For the first two or three days of leaving harbour we would have fresh food, but again all we would have would be a domestic refrigerator, which we would have jammed in with fresh meat, that's all, once that had gone, and it would last for about two days, we were then living on tinned food. Corned beef, tinned meat, sausages, tinned sausages, plenty of fresh vegetables. We did have beef screen for quite a while. That's a screen which is on the upper deck which is equivalent to a wardrobe, you might say, with a metal mesh all the way round, into which would be hung the meat which would be for the whole ship's company. So that once that had gone we had to then live on tinned food. We had potatoes, plenty of potatoes, plenty of greens, all that sort of thing. So it was up to the ingenuity of the cook as to how he could vary the food. (*Dykes*)

From the food point of view, that wasn't particularly good, because although we probably did get more rations than the civilian people, you were very restricted with galley space and with what you could carry. Most of the food would be sort of what you would call today [tinned food], marrowfat peas, beans, haricot beans. You'd get flour. Once you'd gone to sea your fresh meat wouldn't last more than two or three days, so fresh stuff, including bread, after two or three days you'd be out of that sort of thing. You'd have to return to hard tac [originally ship's biscuits but used here as a generic term for tinned food]. All sorts of ways of cooking corned beef, of course, and tinned sausages, Maconichies, which was a sort of tin of stew really for want of a better description. Herrings-in [Herrings in tomato sauce], tinned tomatoes, all that sort of thing. It was very difficult really to make food last out. (*Drummond*)

The provision on corvettes for fresh food was very, very limited. After three days there would be no fresh food available at all. Tinned and dehydrated food was the order of the day. I did try on one occasion experimenting, in that I ordered the maximum amount of fresh meat, and using a spare locker we laid down fresh meat, layers of salt, and a weight to try and get pressed beef. This was only partially successful. (*Hollinshed*)

HMS Clover, *a mess provisions locker, 1942* (*courtesy David Enright*)

HMS Orchis, *peeling 'spuds', c. 1944 (courtesy Cyril Stephens)*

The food wasn't all that great. And, of course, because we used to toss about a lot the amount of food you could put up was rather limited. In other words, it was usually, what we call, a pot mess, where everything you had was just stuck in this big pot, hung up on a hook in the mess, therefore it swayed backwards and forwards. Well, it didn't sway, the ship swayed backwards and forwards underneath it, and then you just went up with a mug and dug that in and had that. Originally [we had bread with it], but the bread used to go off as well, used to go mouldy, so that probably lasted about three or four days and then you went on to biscuits, hard biscuits. (*Grant*)

Mostly when it was rough it was always stew. I always remember it because it used to be in a great big iron sort of pot thing and it would be hung upon a hammock hook so that it didn't swash about too much, you know, and bale it out of there. I think our worst job was bread. We had a job with the bread. After about three days it would go mouldy. We did have a cook who could cook a bit of bread, so it weren't too bad. (*Stephens*)

There was always tins of herrings-in and tinned sausages and all that kind of stuff. We had rum at eleven o'clock, and that was good. One thing I can always remember about being on board the old *Orchis*, if we had a cold my friend Bobby Logan, his mother used to send him jars of honey and shortbread, she lived in Kircudbright. And if we had a cold we used to get a tot of rum, a lump of butter, take it up to the galley and let the cook hot it up for us, and get it down us while it was hot – shift anything that would. (*Stephens*)

They decided to give us refrigerators. We got a 7 cubic foot domestic refrigerator for a crew of seventy for twenty-five days. Totally inadequate. In the wintertime, of course, you'd just hang [meat] on the rigging and leave it frozen. (*Chesterman*)

When we were going to Newfoundland, that was a bit of a bonus when we were over there, because when we got over there we could buy lots of tinned fruit, tinned juices. Things like that, which, of course, you couldn't get in the United Kingdom, so that was a bit of a bonus. (*Grant*)

The engine room were far better off than us, because the galley was just atop of the hatch that leads down to the engine room, whereas in our case we had to go pretty near two-thirds of the way up the ship, for'ard to the galley and then back again. [We ate] on the mess-deck. We had one table for the stokers' mess on the starboard side and another table on port side for'ard for seamen and miscellaneous rates. (*Hallam*)

She had a coal galley; we used to have to 'coal ship'. 'Coal the galley' when you arrived in port. There's a little manhole on the deck, and they'd lift up the manhole and all the seamen or whoever was off duty would have to go and 'coal ship'. You know, all running up and down the gangway with bags of coal on your shoulder, trying to get it down through this little hole, this coal hole, manhole, where they kept it all. (*Jolly*)

Chef had one of the hardest jobs, I would think, on a corvette. No doubt about it. He had a very small galley – if he'd got three pans on top of the range then that was as much as he could do. A very small oven. And most of the times we had hot pot. We always had something on top there, in a massive great big receptacle. We were limited to what we could carry, like meat. About four days and that was that, veg the same thing, about three or four days and that was gone. So then you went back to the old tinned stuff. And chef used to do marvels with some of these tins – his own concoctions. We were on hard tac biscuits, and somehow or other he used to manage to get them soft. I don't know how he did it, but that's what we were reduced to. (*Hallam*)

We always had fiddles on the table, i.e. a section of wood which would cordon off one's plate and mug in order to prevent it sliding on the deck. This, of

HMS Poppy, *Ben the 'Tanky' sawing meat, North Atlantic, 1944* (courtesy Ted Kirby)

course, did not prevent it at all times. Sometimes it finished up on the deck-head. The steward coped, and coped very well, and looked after us very well. (*Hollinshed*)

I suppose the worst part really was the food. We were what was called canteen messing. That meant to say that each mess was allocated a certain sum of money, so you purchased your own food. If you spent all your money within the month, well it was just hard luck. You could go into debt slightly, but it wasn't a particularly good thing to do. There was no cold rooms on these ships, no fridges, so the fresh food that we used to buy in Londonderry, usually after about four or five days, had either been exhausted or had gone bad. The potatoes in fact were kept on the upper deck just above the funnel, and the salt spray and the fumes from the funnel didn't do them much good. So we used to run out of fresh food after about four days. We used [then] to live on tinned food, which was mainly stews and that sort of thing, which you got from cans. None of us had any experience of catering or cooking. We used to have to prepare all our meals and they were taken up to the galley where the one ship's cook cooked them. And if you put, say, a shin of beef up as a roast, he cooked it. Even though he should have said, 'You can't roast this.' But that was what this chap was like. He also cooked for the officers' mess as well. And, as I say, no one was experienced in catering. (*Grant*)

We were canteen messing. And canteen messing means that you go to the stores [you purchase your own provisions and two of you are] allocated as cooks of the mess a week. You go to the stores, you get the food, bring it back, prepare it and you take it up to the galley on deck where the chef will cook it for you. But we always had fresh meat. We had white bread because it was baked up there. And, as a matter of fact, it was a bit wasteful because we didn't have any refrigeration and any meat over had to go over the side or something like that, or [you'd] go round catching sharks with it with a big hook. But the food was good, and I didn't have any problems at all. (*Donkin*)

Messing was strictly speaking a type that they used to call 'canteen messing'. The Navy provided basic things – butter, bread, and meat – when it was available, and we then got a small allowance. I'm not quite certain what it was, but probably something like a shilling a day to buy all the other stuff, which, in a corvette, wasn't very easy because we didn't carry any NAAFI [Navy, Army and Air Force Institutes] canteen, and in a destroyer a NAAFI canteen would have provided all the other bits and pieces which the messes then in turn bought. So on a corvette your only opportunity of buying all those sort of things would have been in harbour, where there would have been probably a local NAAFI, or by bartering over the ship's side, if you were in places like Londonderry, Gibraltar, any of those sort of places, you could have bought the things ashore. And so it was a pretty tight state of affairs when it came to the financial side of it.

The system that evolved: each mess appointed a caterer, who organized the individual messing. He was responsible for the accounting. The accounting was done month to month, so if you had a good mess caterer who looked after his affairs fairly stable, at the end of the time you wouldn't have any money to pay. But if you overshot your money, at the end of the month you may have a few shillings to pay, which wouldn't be very easy in those sort of days. However, each day there was two cooks, what they call 'cooks of messes', who didn't actually do any cooking, but they prepared your particular food. If you had potatoes to peel the cook would peel the potatoes and put them in the net, and they were taken up to the galley where there were official cooks who cooked the food. But the official cook didn't do any preparing at all, all the preparing was done in your own messes by your own particular cooks. And they in turn, when the food was ready, went up to the galley, collected it and served it out in the mess-deck, making certain that the people who were on watch, that their food was either put on plates or taken back up into the ovens. You always had to make certain that all your mates was fed as well. (*Drummond*)

HMS Clematis, *relaxing with a drink of Kye, North Atlantic, 1942* (courtesy Frank Richmond)

Atlantic lifesaver, Kye slab cocoa *(Royal Naval Museum Collection)*

It was an old saying, 'Hands to dinner, CW ratings to lunch.' (*Arthur*)

It was called Kye, and some people would spell it Kia or Kye, which in actual fact was block chocolate, pure cocoa, with like a gritty substance in it, there's always bits of grit in it. And the method of making it was, the person who was going to make it would grate this – it was quite hard – into a jug or pan, and he would mix that up with water as best he could and then boil it up. They always used to say, if you could make it so's the spoon would stand up in it, that was okay for drinking. I've known some people put custard powder in it to liven it up. Some people put rum in it. There's various sort of methods. But it really was pure cocoa. It's the purest cocoa that you could get in slab form. It wasn't so easy to eat, you know, it was bitter to eat, but it made super stuff that stuck to the lining of your stomach, and I think you needed something like that, I think you really needed that on cold nights, something to line your stomach with at that time of the night.

It was an institution in the Navy. 'Go and make the Kye.' Signalmen quite often made it for the bridge, you know. You'd get the stokers who used to make good Kye, because they had steam drains. In corvettes, in particular, you had a nice gadget in the mess. It was a steam coil that came up from the engine room. It was a bit like a central heating system in actual fact. And you'd fill up the jug with water, turn on the steam [and as it went] round the coil, it then 'centrally heated' the water to boiling point, and then you made your tea. But the stokers had a special little drainpipe they used to put in their cocoa and bubble it up that way. They always used to say that the stokers made the best cocoa, or Kye – quite unusual. (*Drummond*)

They had bars on the range. There was bars there that had slotted into place so they just went with the roll. But we nearly always had Kye. We had these big slabs of chocolate, cocoa. There was always one of those on the stove. That was pretty regular. You could send the stoker from the boiler room with his little kettle and he used to top it up and bring it back down and the same with the engine room. (*Hallam*)

Everyday there was the pipe 'up-spirits' and the representative from the mess would go down, and the coxswain would say, 'How many people today, seven?', and he'd get seven tots. Now it was supposed to be that Chief Petty Officers got theirs neat, and we had had to have ours watered down two to one. But being a small ship we were trusted to water down our own tot, which, of course, we never did. And it's fairly potent stuff. I don't know what the size was, but I should think it's as good as a double, maybe 80 proof. It was totally forbidden, but we all did it, to bottle your tot. You got a bottle before you started, you put your rum into this bottle and you got it full before you got to the other side. The rumour was that you put a couple of sultanas in it, or raisins, it improved the flavour. But when you got to the far side and went alongside the American oiler, whose crew knew very well what the score was, and a little bit of bartering went on for whatever it was you were interested in for the rum, and that was terribly forbidden. And nobody could do anything about it as far as I know. The leading hand, who was a very nice man, he was a three-badge man, which meant he'd been fifteen years in. Now a leading hand of fifteen years, you're a bit suspicious about that. He should be a Petty Officer, but we saw why, because he drank his rum, having bottled it, and he went paralytic for a couple of days. And we all had to look after him and everybody knew what happened. The wardroom knew this happened and we had a little working arrangement, I think I'm right, that we just kept him out of sight as much as possible. So that's what one did on board, you looked after each other. (*Arthur*)

We had our own spirit locker in the wardroom. You had beer, which was bottled, spirits, and the ship's company, they would have up-spirits every morning. (*Dykes*)

There were always people who suffered quite severely from seasickness. It was quite sad really to see some people who suffered day in and day out. It was very difficult for them to carry out their particular duties. But there was always another chap who would take his place. It certainly wasn't easy. It was very difficult to get food down . . . in the corvette that I was in we were fortunate, we had an extended fo'c's'le, but some corvettes didn't have that so they had to go from the galley, across an open deck space and quite often the food was getting drowned, you might say, by the seas that were coming over the ship's side. But it wasn't easy to get food from a to b, because you had ladders to go down and take it down to the mess. Once you got down to the mess you had to invariably hang your pot of stew, you might say, from a piece of string, you know, so's it swung with the ship. Otherwise it would have gone straight off the table onto the deck and you would have lost it. (*Drummond*)

I was always vulnerable to seasickness, strangely enough, having been at sea all my life, and I recall on one occasion having so many clothes on and being so weak from seasickness, I could hardly mount the companion way to get onto the bridge. I was so physically weak, and I think that the crew retired quickly when there was no daylight. The food was poor. We were reeling all the time. You couldn't cook anything, you see, tinned soup or whatever you like. If we cooked any meat it would be like leather, because we hung it on deck. It was frozen and we put it in the fridge to thaw, not the other way about. (*Atkinson*)

'A Bucket of Water'
WASHING DOWN AND WRAPPING UP

I said to the bloke, 'Where do you wash down?' He said,
'In here.' I said, 'What do you do for water then?' He
said, 'Go up the galley; get a bucket of water.' You went up
the galley, had to pump up with a semi-rotary pump up in
the galley in a big tank, and you went up there with your
bucket, opened it up in front of the geyser, and got a bucket
of water and just stood there and washed down.

JOLLY

North Atlantic. It was very cold. The facilities? Like water? We just about made enough water. We only had one evaporator on board and we just about made enough water to feed the boilers and for the chef to do the cooking, what little he could do. The taps were locked; you couldn't use them. You could wash first thing in the morning and that was it. No way could you have a bath or anything like that. The taps were locked. Nobody shaved; you couldn't shave. You can imagine we looked a pretty sight after six weeks. You did smell a bit. (*Hallam*)

We had a bathroom, a bath, washbasin, but we had our own wash cabinet in the cabins. So that except for bathing there was no need to use the bathroom. There was a separate ship's head, officers' heads at the top of the accommodation ladder. It was quite adequate. We shared the galley with the ship's company. There was a small wardroom pantry where we had a steward who looked after us all. (*Dykes*)

There was, of course, a very limited supply of fresh water carried, and this was really kept for drinking purposes only, and cooking. Washing was with sea water, which wasn't very comfortable. Sea water was also piped round the ship for washing down decks, so there were hydrants and things like that. The washbasin in the cabin, as I remember, was a kind of cabinet with a stainless steel bowl, and a steward would bring a jug of water which you would pour in and wash. Very basic. There was a bathroom, of course, but bathing in sea water, it's not pleasant. So that was only used in harbour time. And washing clothes, of course. On the lower deck they all wash their own in buckets of soapy water which they call 'soogy' and, of course, as officers we had the privilege of a steward washing our clothes, which was rather nice. (*Richmond*)

They were a bit basic, the heads, although it was virtually a sort of toilet seat with a pair of flapping doors. Every roll of the ship, they flapped backwards and forwards. The washing facilities were fairly basic, too. We had no baths as such. We just had round circular tin baths for bathing in, and some ships had a shower, but washing facilities were very basic. (*Drummond*)

Just up above, before you went out onto the deck, I think there was about three toilets, as many as that, and a washbasin, a couple or three washbasins. And if you wanted a shower you got a bucket of water and pushed it up on top of your head for a shower. You pump your water. (*Stephens*)

We did have a chief stoker who used to cut hair for a tanner, for sixpence, you know. And you might be in the first dog at sea, and he'd say, 'Right, anybody want a haircut? I'm doing them down on fo'c's'le, down on the quarter deck.' And he'd be sat there on a stool and he'd be cutting hair. But you'd have it cut, you know. (*Jolly*)

Every man used to have a galvanized bucket which he kept as his personal bucket, and he kept this very clean – only used it for washing clothes in, see. So he washed the clothes in this bucket and then, after rinsing, you rung them out and you could then hang them up on lines which were put above the boiler room of the ship. So very rarely did you have the opportunity of drying them in the open air. Usually everyone used the boiler room to do the washing. (*Grant*)

They would hand wash all their clothing. There were no washing facilities, no mechanical washing facilities, all hand washing. And, of course, one did not hang one's washing out on a line on the upper deck [but] in confined passageways, which would enable it to drip dry, if not dry. These, of course, had to be removed for captain's rounds in harbour. (*Hollinshed*)

It was great in the engine room because that was where, if you wanted anything dried, you'd have a word with the chief stoker or whoever it was [on watch], and you could hang things up in the warm engine room, which was always very warm and smelling of oil, and it was a sort of little inferno. (*Arthur*)

[We wore] whatever you could lay your hands on: jumper, jerseys. The Admiralty were quite good. When we did the Arctic run they issued us with pure wool long johns, but I don't think anybody kept them, and certainly nobody wore them, 'cos they itched. Oh, God, they itched! They were virgin wool – hadn't even had the lanolin taken out, and they used to smell horrible. When they got warm, on your body, oh, you used to smell like an old sheep. Oh, terrible! I think most of the lads flogged 'em to the dockyard mateys in Belfast. We were in there for a refit and they flogged 'em to the dockyard mateys, and we went without them. (*Goldsmith*)

HMS Poppy, *washing on the fo'c's'le, North Atlantic, 1943. Jim Mann, telegraphist, is at the bucket; Les Floyd, signalman, is on the left* (courtesy Ted Kirby)

Normally overalls [were worn] – the blue dungaree, complete blue overalls they used to serve out in the service. Sometimes [the top part] was rolled down and the sleeves tied round the waist so you only had the bottom half on. Some used to wear grey flannel trousers who'd come in [hostilities only crew]. Of course, we didn't have any – the regulars, but they used to wear their civilian clothes, well civilian trousers. And we were always clomping around in sea boots and that sort of thing. You had the duffle-coat for cold weather. But you also had oilskins. You had an oilskin coat, oilskin leggings and you also had sea boots. Towards the end of my time on [board] there, they brought in a very good thing actually. It was what you would these days call a survival suit. It was an overall suit which would button up, but had a thick layer of kapok in it. In fact they were so warm, even in the coldest weather the only thing you needed to wear underneath was just your underwear. But they weren't waterproof in the sense that an oilskin were. They would keep water out but they were very much like the material you get these days, the showerproof material. (*Grant*)

There was the usual blue sailor's uniform which you learned to put on. This suit has a serge collar on top of which you placed the blue jean collar with its

HMS Snowflake, *1943. Left to right: George Ambler, Maurice Smeaton, Cyril Hatton and Les Taylor* (*courtesy Cyril Hatton*)

three white-striped edging. The bottom of this was tucked under the jumper at the waist and tied with tape. But when you were aboard at night you changed into night clothing, which meant you removed the blue jean collar leaving the serge collar of your jumper exposed. Under your serge jumper you wore a white cotton drill 'front' which had a square-neck edging of blue jean tape which was worn in summer. In winter you wore a blue service jersey. (*Drummond*)

Unfortunately, the blue dye would run into the white tapes and that was terrible, so you had that sort of little problem. There were old hands who could tell you how to cope with that. But on top of that you wore, not a duffle-coat, that was a bit of class, the duffle-coats were limited, the leading hands would have a duffle-coat and you'd finish up in something like a teddy bear suit, made in a sort of mackintosh. But nearly always you'd be wearing your naval uniform with a jersey underneath and a sweater and an oilskin. Now an oilskin was heavy black, it didn't bend, and to climb up into the crow's nest in an oilskin was quite a feat. (*Arthur*)

Richard Grant, HMS Polyanthus, *Atlantic, 1941* (*courtesy Richard Grant*)

Duffle-coats were worn with an assortment of headgear, but the most difficult provision was in keeping, or preventing the water trickling down one's neck. A variety of things were worn – scarves, towels – anything to try and prevent the water trickling down one's neck – mostly unsuccessful. (*Hollinshed*)

If it was wet, you know, raining, you'd be dressed in a pair of sea boots, a pair of heavy sea boot stockings, coat, a mackintosh coat on top of that, a sou'wester, a towel tied round your neck, a pair of gloves and a pair of binoculars, and you clamber up this crow's nest and get inside it. It was like a steel tub, and it was just enough . . . your eyes would just go to the top, and the wind used to cut. You could hardly see. But the worst thing of all if you were crow's nest lookout is when you had a following sea, when the fumes from the funnel used to come over the top of the crow's nest, and if you weren't sick by the time you got up there you were sick from the fumes . . . awful. (*Stephens*)

But most of the time, of course, when you turned in you didn't take your clothes off. You might take your sea boots off, but the rest of the time – because when action stations went you didn't have any time at all – you didn't take your clothes off. I remember taking my sea boot stockings off after a trip and my legs inside were totally white and smelling of ammonia, because of the decomposition products coming through, and it came out as ammonia. (*Arthur*)

[We] always laid there fully dressed, without the boots, of course. We'd put our sea boots on when there was an alarm called or we were going on watch. We'd come out and we had what we called a 'goon suit' – a one-piece waterproof suit which was I think kapok-lined – which was very warm. So we used to get into that, button up in that, boots, I used to wear a towel round the neck to stop water going in, and a sou'wester. And like that we'd keep moderately dry whilst on watch. (*Richmond*)

CHAPTER FIVE

OFF-WATCH

Invariably, I think, people would either be playing cards or playing crib, or telling stories, that sort of thing.

Geoffrey Drummond, RN, 1938–1973;
Torpedo Coxswain, HMS CAMPION

For the crews of the corvettes, there was very little time to spare. When they were not on watch or taking care of the ship, they would try to sleep. However, they did find some small time for amusement. Mostly they would play cards. Nearly all appreciated tot-time, which became a general moment for socializing. Some would engage in general bantering games with each other; some would even go for long runs. Others participated in a more irreverent sport: fishing with depth-charges.

Layovers abroad often meant visiting bars and meeting women, although sex, apparently, especially aboard ship, was not an overwhelming preoccupation. Occasionally, layovers meant a time for rest and relaxation in the home of some locals; generally it meant a time to secure precious goods for family members back home. Indeed, the consideration of family members at home was a central concern. They kept in touch with each other by letters, the writing of which occupied many. Sometimes the crew members would arrive home, bearing gifts they had brought back from abroad, long before their letters arrived.

For the most part, though, off-watch was a time when gentle distractions, often cloaked in humour, made the reality of their precarious existences more bearable. The characters, the jokes and banter – often sexual – even the pets they occasionally kept aboard, helped make life a little less stark, a little more humane.

'Time to Spare'

AT PLAY

Recreation? If there was any time to spare, it would be used for playing uckers {ludo}, or the one where you have the little board with men going up and down – cribbage. Cribbage was the one that was played a great deal on board. Much the same as any other family when it's raining and they can't go out, so what do they do, they find entertainment amongst themselves.

ARTHUR

When you were off-watch in harbour during the day, you turned to and did a bit of work like cleaning ship. And then at night, if you were liberty men, you'd go ashore and the duty watch was left on board to clear up mess and [attend to] any emergencies that might arise. But you had lots and lots of hobbies, you know, when you were at sea. I remember I used to be a dab hand

HMS Honeysuckle, *Carley float racing, off Iceland, June 1941* (*courtesy Dick Dykes*)

with the needle, doing a bit of embroidery, or sewing badges on, useful way to cadge an extra tot of rum. If a fellow had, say, a good conduct badge or he'd passed for leading seaman and he wanted his badge sewn on a bit tiddly, you know, not with a cobbler's stitch, sort of style, but nice and neat, you know. If you could sew it on for him, and then we'd say, 'Well, it'll cost you a tot.' But one thing we used to do which was very popular on board the *Orchis*, the collars with the three white lines on. [These were collars with three white tapes around the collar edge and issued as part of the uniforms to all ordinary seamen. (Dykes)] They were always machine-stitched when we had them off the ODs [Ordinary Seaman], and what we used to do, we used to strip the white tape off the collars, boil the collars till they got lovely pale blue, and then we used to buy some tape and we used to stitch some tape on those collars, lovely. Jack then, when [he] went ashore you know, [he] didn't seem as if [he'd] just joined, [he'd] been to sea. (*Stephens*)

Off-watch time, we played cards. We had various games we used to play. Some of them were very silly and very dangerous. There was one particular game that I and the leading telegraphist used to play when we were off-watch. We used to stick our sheath knives in the mess-deck table, mine with the edge facing him and his with his edge facing mine, stick them in the table about an inch apart, and then we used to put a piece of string between them and he'd hold one end in his mouth and I'd hold one end in my mouth and we'd try and pull each other onto the knife blades. (Laughs) I mean, you could very easily get a cut nose. I made sure I never got my nose cut; I let go at the last minute – chicken, you know. But that was one of the daft things. The other daft thing that some of them used to do [was to] spread their hands on the mess-deck table and [then] they'd see how fast they could stab a knife point between their fingers. That was fraught, of course, I mean, if they weren't absolutely dead accurate – minus a finger, very quickly, or a badly cut finger. Mostly, [though, we played] cards I suppose, or writing home, if we could write; if it wasn't too rough. Or sleeping, catching up on sleep. Mostly it was catching up on sleep, because your sleep was so often disturbed by action stations and or the weather again, that you just grabbed a kip whenever you could, you know, to catch up. (*Goldsmith*)

Usually we played cards, or dominoes, whatever. [There was] little else to do. You couldn't walk up and down the upper deck or anything of that sort. So we just played cards, as I say, and ludo or dominoes or something like that. (*Hallam*)

One particular captain used to like to get hold of [woollen] jerseys and pick them to pieces and put them into the officers' bath. Any colour, well, light colours white or grey, and then dye them a particular colour, green usually or blue. The bath was a horrible colour. And then he would get all this wool out of the bath and dry it off in the boiler room. And then when he'd got that, he'd unpick a canvas sack and make himself a rug. He was making rugs; I made rugs. The ratings would draw, play games, cards, good old 'uckers' it was known as. We had to make our own activity. Read, that was about the best thing to do really, go to your cabin and read. (*Dykes*)

There was a great deal of handicraft, too. People would be making things. Not knitting so much but making rugs. There was a general tradition on the mess-deck of handicraft that some people were good at and some people weren't. There was very much a self-contained busy time. There was something called a 'make-and-mend', which was given occasionally, which meant you had the afternoon off. Make-and-mend when you made and mended your own uniform. Original naval uniforms were made by the sailors themselves. And there were still one or two people on board who would take it upon themselves to do your repairs for you. There was a little chap who was known to be a tailor or something. He would do a little bit of tailoring work if you wanted to take your jumper in, or [whatever]. And there was another chap who was excellent at washing those wretched collars and getting them lighter and whiter. Money, you paid him. He said, 'I will do this; it will cost you so much.' People ran little firms on board. (*Arthur*)

Perhaps he'd cut the captain's hair that day, because once he found out that he could do it, that was it. And so if they had a fine day and he wasn't on duty, then he used to be on deck cutting the crews' hair, keeping them tidy. (*Helen Canham*)

If you're at sea you didn't drink, in that sense. Tot-time was accepted, but I think tot-time was a good thing. It was a time when, probably the only time in the day or the night, when people endeavoured to get together. They were all together. It was a social point, a meeting point. A warm occasion you might say, you know, to be there for the issue of the grog, and if you'd got a mate who'd done you a favour, he got a sippers or gulpers, it depended on the extent of the favour. I mean, all those things were good things, I think. (*Drummond*)

A gang of us decided that perhaps it would be nice if we could go out for a run in the morning, and so you'd got to get permission from the officer of the watch to leave the ship. Six or seven of us started it off, and in the finish we were getting about thirty of the ship's company going out for a run in the morning. We'd be going out through the streets of Hull, all over the place we used to go. I remember once in Newfoundland we went out one morning. It was blowing a blizzard; well, the snow was horizontal so you can tell how [bad it was]. The Newfoundlanders were going along with a great big hood over their heads, you know, muffled up, and we went by with a pair of shorts and a singlet on. They must have thought we were mad. We were, but we were fit, you see. If you're fit you're living in a different world. (*Stephens*)

When we used to leave the convoys on the Grand Banks just near Newfoundland, on the way to St John's, we would drop a depth-charge over the stern and stun the fish. And so we'd then lower a dinghy and pick up possibly a hundred very nice cod, large cod, and so the photographs show the cod being gutted by two

HMS Alisma, *Donald Canham cutting hair, North Atlantic, 1941–3* (*courtesy Helen Canham*)

HMS Honeysuckle, *collecting cod stunned by depth-charges off St John's*, c. 1942
(courtesy Dick Dykes)

expert fishermen we had on board – in fact they were Newfoundlanders, and they would gut our fish for us. They had the knowledge and the speed in which to do it. (*Dykes*)

Well, when you dropped a depth-charge, supposing you were on the way home and they were going to exercise with the depth-charges, the asdic people would probably pick up a shoal of fish, and you'd whip a depth-charge over the side and, as soon as you see the old seagulls descend, you'd 'Away sea boat's crew.' And we'd go along and pick up these fish and bring them inboard. And we had a fellow on board, Leadbetter [by name], who was a deep-sea fisherman pre-war, and he used to glory in gutting these fish. And you had to be careful when passing him by because you'd probably get a fish's inside slung at you. But to get that fish into the galley within an hour of being gutted, and fried, it was out of this world. There's nothing like it. (*Stephens*)

We used to love it when we went out on exercises and dropped depth-charges round the coast of Derry. Because before we started, the captain used to say, 'Right put one of the ship's boats away.' And they used to go and pick all the fish up, because it used to stun the fish and they'd all float up to the top, and it was fish and chips for dinner that night. But, you know, it wasn't all doom and gloom. There was a lot of good times, a lot of fun. (*Goldsmith*)

'A Lot of Stockings'

LAYOVERS

*The last time he was across the Atlantic, I suppose, he'd
got a big tea chest and he'd got this full of all sorts of
things for different people, you know, and I had to dole it
all out. Necklaces for some of them, anything, stockings.
He used to bring a lot of stockings.*

HILDA STEPHENS

We would then go to a base in Newfoundland called Argentia, which was a
lease-lend base to the Americans in exchange for the fifty destroyers they lent
us to help us with the escort duties. This base was really basic. It had a few
Nissen huts when we first saw it. In fact, it was typically British naval world,
temporary place. But when the Americans came, first of all they had a huge
depot ship there, the *Prairie*, with machine-shop facilities, all kinds of
facilities on board. And then, of course, they built clubs for the men and
clubs for the officers, and we had cinemas and every kind of imaginable
facility. So it became a magnificent base. (*Richmond*)

Now Argentia, in Newfoundland, was a very small original village or town,
of wooden houses, with an enormous American naval base. And when you

Fisherman's Creek, St John's, Newfoundland (courtesy Ted Kirby)

went ashore, there was nothing to do. You walked to Argentia – I think the village was about 2 or 3 miles away – and you went to the store and you bought up things like bananas and tinned meat, and things to bring home. The bananas were quite interesting because the only way to carry bananas safely is in the cool. And I found a place in the chain locker, for'ard. And I used to have all my bananas hanging up in the chain locker. Well, nobody really knew about it, and [the bananas] never actually came up when we dropped anchor, which I was always worried about, that they'd come up with the cable. But Argentia, you'd be there for two or three days and then you'd go off again. It wasn't much fun. Halifax was great; St John's not bad, but it was nearly always Argentia, and you thought, oh my God, Argentia. And so you'd go back again. (*Arthur*)

Going into Newfoundland there were shops there. There were all the goods and foodstuffs which were on rations or in short supply here and there they were plentiful. They were near Canada and America and the shops were stocked as normal. And, of course, the great thing for the girlfriend was nylon stockings; that was one of the first things we used to stock up on. And big tins of ham I can remember, and I think cloth and other clothes and things we used to stock up. So we had tremendous . . . what we used to call 'rabbits'. 'Rabbits' was the naval term for all this kind of stuff you bought for taking ashore. (*Richmond*)

[We would buy] a lot of things. Pyrex would be an item, Witney blankets was another one, many things like that. Material for curtains, things which we found would be available in the stores in Water Street of St John's after a few days when the ships had unloaded. The staff of these stores would tell us that 'We'd got nice blankets in' which were available. (*Dykes*)

[You] usually [had] only about three or four days [layover in Halifax]. You'd paint ship, chip paint or work on your housekeeping. You were working quite hard to get the ship ready to go to sea again. You'd be loading more depth-charges, if you used any. You'd certainly be loading good shipping stores. You were kept quite busy in those days. If you went ashore there wasn't a great deal to do. If you went ashore you'd get back on board by eleven o'clock. Most of the time we'd go for a meal or something like that. In Halifax there'd be one or two clubs for ratings to go ashore, keep out of mischief. (*Arthur*)

It was really a case of making our own recreation for the short period of time. Go to the local bars – they don't have pubs over there they have bars. You go

HMS Poppy. *Stokers from the crew sledge outside St John's, 1945* (*courtesy Ted Kirby*)

and get your liquor from the liquor store and take it to the bars and drink it there.

Sex was not a real preoccupation on board. Of course, there was always the 'Golden Rivet' [laughs]. No, really, we had so much to preoccupy our minds – watches, concerns about families, survivors. We were in too close quarters for it to preoccupy us. We were more concerned to get home on leave or to get ashore to enjoy ourselves. (*Dykes*)

When we got ashore, we tended to head for bars where there was women. In the run to the States, there was no shortage of women. In Novia Scotia the locals were always friendly. In Liverpool there was great scope for meeting members of the opposite sex. There was fourteen days or so between trips. VD was only a great danger when we were in a place for a long time. The Grafton Ballroom, that was a meeting point in Liverpool.

I don't recall there was much homosexuality. There was those who were called-up. Usually they opted for jobs like stewards or sick-berth attendants. In those days it was a bit more of a secretive matter. (*Drummond*)

In St John's we had what was known in the Navy, and I'm sure it probably still is, 'up-homers'. Now 'up-homers' is if you could get in with a civilian family that would invite you up their home, hence 'up-homers'. St John's had a very good scheme. They had a sort of services organization there, something like the Sailor's Rest idea here, and they had a scheme whereby, if you wanted to meet any of the local people, you'd put your name down, whether you like a drink or not, or teetotal or whatever, and they would then pass [your name] on to any of the locals that came in and wanted to entertain a couple of matelots, you see. Well, we debated, we said if we put down that we like a drink we won't get [invited] you see, in the end we decided we'd put down, 'we like a drink'; we're not the only ones in the world that like a drink, beer or something, so we put all this down. And we were told to come back a couple of evenings later, and we sat there waiting and various civilians came in and picked up a sailor here and a sailor there, and we got almost to the end of the queue. There was only us and a few others left, and then this man walked in. I think he was probably the most ugly man I've ever seen. He looked as though his face had been trodden on by an elephant. Really ugly man. And I sort of jokingly said, 'Bet we've got him,' you see, and we did, it was us. Well, he turned out the nicest man I've met in many a long day. He was a Liverpool chap and he'd gone over and married a Newfoundland girl and worked over there, and those people they weren't well-off by any means, but they treated us like royalty. (*Goldsmith*)

HMS Snowflake, *the jerry-rigged swimming pool on the fo'c's'le, 1944. Howard Goldsmith is fifth from the right* (courtesy Howard Goldsmith)

When we were based in Greenock and Gourock, we used to take the little train up to Glasgow, and the first port of call was Glasgow Empire. I loved the theatres and all the shows then. We were lucky because one of our members' wives worked in the ticket office at Glasgow Empire, and so she had a rough idea of when we would be home and so she used to hang on to a few tickets just in case, and so we saw some wonderful shows up there. And I remember once Maurice Wilikin's *Daughters of Lovelace* were appearing and one of the stewards came down during the interval and said they wanted two sailors to lead Britannia down the steps for the grand finale. And I said, 'Right, that's me.' So I went up with another one of our ship's company and we lead Britannia down the steps, and so I can honestly say I appeared on Glasgow Empire stage.

I used to love London. We did a refit in East Ham once and we used to go up to London and go to the theatres up there. And one of the things I loved about it, because there were six of us who used to hang about together, and we went down Shaftesbury Avenue on the lookout for some food and we came across an old café there. The windows were broken and old curtains, so we piled in there and there was a dear old lady behind the counter with white hair. 'What do you lads want?' We said, 'Steak, eggs and chips', and she said, 'You can have steak eggs and chips.' Well, that shook us for a start, you know. It was one of those cafés where the kitchen must have been downstairs, because you shouted down a hole and it came up on a trolley affair, you know.

HMS Circassia, SODS Opera, *off Gibraltar, 1940. Frank Richmond is in the middle row, far right* (courtesy Frank Richmond)

And all the time we were there and we went ashore we went to that place, and we used to take the old girl some cigarettes and chocolate if we had any to spare. And years after the war, when the war was over, the wife and myself we went to London to a theatre and I said, 'Let's go down Shaftesbury Avenue and see if that old café is still there.' Well, it was. The window had been repaired and the curtains had been washed, and we went in and this dear old lady was still there, so we ordered a meal and when I went up to pay she looked at me hard. She said, 'I've seen you somewhere before.' I said, 'Well, I don't come from these parts I come from Gloucestershire.' She said, 'Your face is familiar, I've seen you somewhere before.' 'Oh, have you,' I said, 'I wonder where that could have been then?' I tittered on a bit more, then I said, 'Can you remember the six sailors who used to . . .', 'Ah, that's it,' she said. But I went up a couple of years later and I suppose the poor old dear had passed away, [because her café] was done up to the nines; the atmosphere had gone. But she was a lovely old lady. (*Stephens*)

'Home Safely'

FAMILIES

*Just the hope that at the end of the war he would come
home safely to us. We just used to read the newspapers
and listen to the news. I think it was the news that kept
us informed more than anything. Yes, we listened to all
the news bulletins, just to hear what was happening.*

IRIS DYKES

When you were at sea you'd probably write letters for, you know, for posting when you got into harbour. (*Stephens*)

No, we didn't get mail until we got back to the United Kingdom. There was never any mail in St John's for us because there was no way of getting it there quicker than we would get there. But when we got home we would have twenty days', thirty days' mail waiting for us, so it was a busy time.

If, for instance, we had a destroyer or two with us, because we'd been hard pressed and they were leaving for home, they would say to us, 'If you've got any mail, we'll take it.' So we would write a quick note. In about 25 minutes or an hour's time, it'd be put in the mailbag and passed over to the destroyer on a line. They'd just fire a line across to the destroyer and they'd haul it aboard. That's basically how it used to be done. Or when we were in St John's, we'd write a letter; it might get back before we did. On the other hand, we might even take it back with us through a Merchant ship [we were escorting]. Oh yes, we were always writing. (*Dykes*)

They used to bring it down in a launch, the mail, when you came into harbour, bring it in a big sack. It would be in different mess-decks; read it all out, you know. [A petty officer would] come down with the postman, the bloke who got made postman, and they'd shout out different names. All the blokes used to muster together and sort of wait to be called, you know. But it was always exciting when you got mail. (*Jolly*)

We used to get, what they called, a privilege envelope. I can't remember how many you used to get, but something like one or two a month, and the privilege envelope, if you wrote that it was not to be opened by the censor, you were taken on trust that you weren't giving away information. But all other letters would have been censored on board, and they were censored by the ship's officers. They used to take it in turns, reading all the sailors' mail, crossing out bits that shouldn't be there. (*Grant*)

[My family] would send me a letter occasionally and I would send them a postcard occasionally, but most of the time you were six weeks between contact. You certainly didn't get any mail. I don't think there was any mail delivered to the other side [of the Atlantic] because there would be no time for it to get across. I'm fairly certain we had ship's mail brought round when we got back to harbour and the boat would come alongside with the mail. And you'd get all your letters at one go every six weeks. But keeping in touch with the family was when you went on leave, I suppose. You might have four or five days' leave at a time. (*Arthur*)

It was the letters. That's all we had open to us in those days. (*Iris Dykes*)

We had worked out a code of girls' names which meant different places – that was highly secret. That was just between the two of us. So that if he wrote and said he'd seen Alice, I knew he'd gone to one certain place. And, of course, he always hoped – he was a cold sort of person in the fact that he felt the cold – and he hoped that they'd get sent south somewhere but they sent him to Iceland on his first trip.
 Occasionally he got home at a weekend if they got leave. Well, he used to phone me or write to me. I got letters nearly every day, but phone calls as well, and he'd come up as often as he could. I think there was one lieutenant down there who also lived in Southampton, and he used to get a lift with him, sometimes to come home. Otherwise he hitch-hiked. (*Helen Canham*)

A Walt Disney badge made for HMS Oxlip (courtesy John Hollinshed).

'Oxlip *was commissioned in December 1941 with me as her first lieutenant as she lay in a Glasgow shipyard. Notwithstanding the demands of duty during that busy week, I found time on 6 December to get married. The night before my wife and I caught the train for a brief weekend honeymoon in Edinburgh. Sitting with the others over a drink at the hotel, the conversation got around to the war insignia that Walt Disney was reported to be designing for the American bomber crews to display upon the fuselages of their planes. Margaret, my wife, announced that she would write to him to ask him to draw up a suitable badge for* Oxlip. *She also undertook to write to the Royal Horticultural Society to see if they could produce a painting of our name flower. Both applications met with marked success. A few weeks later we received from the Walt Disney studios in Hollywood a magnificent coloured cartoon of Ferdinand the Bull, squatting on his haunches, sniffing delicately at an oxlip. The fact that Walt Disney had put an American sailor's cap between Ferdinand's horns in no way detracted from its suitability, and, when later our artistically inclined leading telegraphist enlarged and copied it on to the side of the 4-inch gun shield, the appropriate correction was made to Ferdinand's headgear. Our ship's escutcheon became famous throughout the Western Approaches escort forces.' (Captain Charles W. Leadbetter, RD)*

I just had to wait until he came home on leave; or, when he got back into port, he used to give me a ring to say he was there and that he was alright. But, apart from that, they used to go for about six weeks across the Atlantic, and just when he got back he used to give me a ring. I think one aged about a hundred years in those days. (*Iris Dykes*)

Otherwise, well, time went very slowly and four years is a long time – five in my case because he didn't come back till, I think it was August '46. Still, I got the home ready. We bought a house and that was ready when he came back.

I don't think he had an official leave; he just came into port and that was it. For refitting or whatever they were doing, and then we used to see each other for three or four days. No, he just turned up. I was always there. There was nothing else to do anyway, just sit in the room. I had a lovely view of the water, midnight sun; it was quite nice. But it was very lonely. (*Edith Hollinshed*)

There was one wife that I used to [see and became] quite friendly with, and her husband was also on one of the 'Flower' class corvettes and we used to compare notes. (*Iris Dykes*)

I did some first-aid, you know. We used to go on duty every so often. And fire-watching when I was at work. We had to do fire-watching. [Where I worked] it was a horrible poky little solicitor's office with all these great big books all covered in dust and it was ever so creepy. But when there was an air raid we used to walk round the block. (*Hilda Stephens*)

I'd already had a picture sent of him in uniform, so I knew what he looked like. But if we went to visit my parents, we went once, and he went out of uniform, and

Geoff Drummond and his grandparents, Morecambe, 1939 (*courtesy Geoff Drummond*)

my father was most disgusted. He said, 'Are you ashamed of it?' So every time after that he had to dress up and put his uniform on so that he could go and see them. (*Helen Canham*)

He used to make me an allowance. It was sent to me but I can't remember what it was. I used to put it away. We used to put it in the bank. And, I suppose, really, I more or less lived on the wages that I earned from work, which wasn't a lot. (*Iris Dykes*)

Oh, yes, he brought some nice things back. Stockings and soap, which was very precious, and fruit, I used to get a lot of fruit as well. Pineapples mainly, huge things, and I think he brought me a melon one time, and chocolate, American chocolate, and that was nice. (*Edith Hollinshed*)

I remember once he brought me home a big hand of bananas, which was quite an event. We had some silk stockings and some underwear, and he brought me home quite a lot of Pyrex ware. (*Iris Dykes*)

Well, there was a lot of people doing it; everybody was doing it. They thought, well, might as well have a few days in case they get bumped off. But we were

Cyril and Hilda Stephens, South Cerney, Gloucestershire, 1993 (*Royal Naval Museum Collection*)

married on the Monday. We went to London for our honeymoon. We went by train and we were on the station for a couple or three hours; just sat on the station, and then presently an express train came through and we learned after that it was Winston Churchill going somewhere or coming back from somewhere, and we had to wait for that train. Everything had to wait; everything stopped until this train had gone through. So I don't know, I think we got to London about four o'clock in the morning. Then we only had about a couple of days even then, and he had to go back to the ship. (*Edith Hollinshed*)

Well, we'd arranged [to get married] one weekend and then his leave was stopped. And when I saw the vicar he said, 'We'll have everything on top line, and then as soon as you know when he's coming home, let me know and we'll arrange it.' So I think it was a Saturday he came home and we were married on the Monday. We'd got it all ready. I'd got the bridesmaids nearly all done. My sister was in the ATS [Auxiliary Territorial Service] and we had to get her home on leave. (*Hilda Stephens*)

'A Little Bit of Informality'

DISTRACTIONS

*But that was the sort of thing that went on – there was
a little bit of informality*

ARTHUR

Oh yes, we had some right boys on board there, you know. When we first commissioned we had rather an acid chap, you know, who thought he was the cat's whiskers. Well, he was a jolly good seaman. He knew his job, but he forgot that we were ordinary civilians who'd come in, ten weeks' training, and he'd probably been in four or five years and had done boy's training and he knew all the ropes. But us poor devils, we got slung in at the deep end. And we had this AB by the name of Tom Cox. He was a bit of a character. He was always in trouble, you know, he was one of the skates and he created what he called his 'foobird'. Well, what it was, he got two potatoes and he made a bird and he put him in like the cage you have on a wandering lead. And he hung it on the hammock hook and he called it his 'foobird', and he used to . . . and he had a little song he used to sing to this thing; he called it his 'foobird' song. And he had a cap ribbon made, HMS *Foo*. He was hilarious. He was like a fatherly figure to us kids. We were kids and as green as grass, and one of the hilarious things about him was, when he used to exercise abandon ship, he'd go to the locker and he'd get hold of a tin of beef and a loaf of bread and he'd fall in with this underneath his arm. But the coxswain had what you call a watch and quarter bill, where, you know, all your duties are put down, and the coxswain had this up on the bulkhead, and he said, 'What, nothing for the 'foobird'? We'll soon alter that,' he said. So he got it off the bulkhead and he put 'foobird' stations for entering harbour, masthead lookout, special duties, whistle while you work, and all such stuff as that. It just took the seriousness out of the job. He was a jolly good seaman too, but a skate because he was always in trouble – always in trouble.

There was one standard trick they used to play. If somebody came on board, a new rating, as soon as we passed Craig Rock the ship used to 'bounce', and we used to look at one another and say, 'Cor! it's getting rough, we'd better have some prayers on the fo'c's'le.' [The new rating would be told] 'Go and get the key of the harmonium.' 'Whose got it?' Well, the coxswain had it. 'Well, go and see the coxswain. Tell him to bring the harmonium so we can start practising.' So away he'd go to the coxswain. 'Oh, he's sorry,' he said. 'The yeoman of signals had that yesterday trying out some new hymns. Go to the yeoman of signals.' And the yeoman of signals would send him to chief stoker. Oh, he never had it; he gave it to the bosun's mate. It was only when he got to the first lieutenant,

Robert Taylor, April 1943, HMS Royal Arthur *(courtesy Robert Taylor)*

you know, he found out that they was pulling his leg. But this was a standard joke about the key of the harmonium. We never had a harmonium on board.

There was [also] a fellow called Simmonds. He was a telegraphist. He was a bit of an eccentric sort of a chappy. He was a bit of a jazz fiend. [There was also] a fellow on board, little Mac, a boy seaman, and Simmonds came down one day smoking a pipe, and so Mac said to him, he said, 'Have you got permission to smoke that pipe?' He said, 'No.' 'Crikey, you should think yourself lucky that you're not put on a charge.' He said, 'You'd better get a request in.' And Simmonds said, 'Some blasted ship this is,' he said. 'You can't smoke a pipe now without putting a request in.' He said, 'You put that request in straight away.' So he got the request – of course, the coxswain and the first lieutenant knew all these dodges. They know all about all these capers. So Simmonds came down to the mess-deck. I was there when he did it. 'Douglas Simmonds requests to see first lieutenant to smoke a pipe.' So it was taken up before the first lieutenant; the request was read out and the first lieutenant said to him, 'Now what tobacco do you propose to smoke in your pipe?' And he said, 'Well, ship's issue and anything I can get ashore.' 'Yes. Do you understand that you've got to smoke this pipe in all winds and weathers.' Yes. He understood that. And he said, 'Furthermore, if you're sick when you're smoking this pipe it's your duty to clean it up. Request granted.'

[I also remember Jasper Hornby]. Once we were going down to Freetown and we passed through the Bay of Biscay and the order was 'Clear lower deck.' Well, that means that everyone who is not on watch on the upper deck. We saw one of our boats, the port boat, was just flapping in the wind like a button on the end of a piece of cotton. It was impossible to secure it, so it was cut loose. We then secured the starboard boat. We hadn't been down below quarter of an hour when again, 'Clear lower decks.' We went up top and the starboard boat, all the Carley floats and every bit of gear we had for lifesaving had gone. Poor Jasper Hornby – I shall always remember Jasper Hornby because, before we left, he picked up with this girl who he said he was going to marry when he got back home. We were going out to Freetown for two years, so Jasper – we called him Jasper – decided to have his hair cut off so that his hair would be lovely when he came home in two years' time, and he also had false teeth. Well, when we got into the Bay of Biscay he lost his teeth over the side through being seasick and he had a long face, similar to Tommy Trinder, and I've never seen anything so hilarious in all my life. Well, the skipper took one look at him, well, he nearly went into hysterics and poor Hornby, see he lost his false teeth, and for all the time we were out in Freetown, luckily we weren't out there for two years, after about six months we got recalled to have an RDF fitted, but poor Hornby, his hair had hardly grown by the time we got back to England. That was one of the things I can remember about Jasper. (*Stephens*)

When we were based at Liverpool there was a publication applicable to Liverpool called *Western Approaches Convoy Instructions*. Every ship had them. Every ship had to have them. And the Confidential Book Officer felt that it was time that every officer should read these and know them off by heart pretty well. So what he did on this particular trip was to hang these forty or fifty looseleaf sheets of paper in the officers' heads on a piece of string. Unfortunately, we had a very active trip and we had a large number of survivors on board, and so naturally they used the officers' heads as well as the ship's company's heads. Well, much to the consternation of the confidential book officer, when we returned to harbour, he found that his *Western Approaches Convoy Instructions* was missing, and so it could only be surmised where it was used. We then had to spend about three or four days testing this paper to see how long it took for it to disintegrate in salt water.

Being in charge on depth-charges, I was responsible for what was called the pistol which goes into the depth-charge and on which you set the depth, which then activates the primer and so forth. Now every pistol had its serial number and every pistol had its history sheet. What I had to do at the end of a trip was, every time we used one of these pistols we had to fill in the history sheet. With the history sheet we had what was called the key, which was in fact the key which came out of the pistol. When you set the depth onto the pistol you pushed the key in and turned it to the appropriate depth and then released it, and the key would come out in your hand. Now that had the serial number of the pistol on it and should relate to the history certificate of the pistol. Now this certificate required me to put the name of the ship, it required me to give the exact position of the ship when the pistol was used and, if I remember rightly, the speed of the ship. And finally, amongst other remarks, but finally, one specific question: what was the explosion like? Well, I do regret to say that I said, 'bang', you see, and all those had to go back to the armament officer with the key and the certificate. What he did with them, I don't know, but I'm quite sure that he'd throw them in the bin, I think, or they're still there to this day. (*Dykes*)

Raymond Donkin (seated), 1944 (courtesy Raymond Donkin)

[At the armament store] I once got the officer of the watch a cup of tea, and this was in a storm. I was bridge messenger, and he said, 'Go and get a cup of tea will you; get one yourself.' So I went down the galley, I drank mine in the galley save carrying two cups up, 'cos she was rolling and I wanted one hand to steady me, so I gave him this cup of tea, and the sea had come over. It took all the tea out and filled it with salt water. I said, 'Here y'are sir,' I said. 'What salt do you have in your tea?' He tasted it and it went straight overboard [laughs]. (*Jolly*)

When I went alongside the oiler at [Moville] once, I was a non-smoker but I drew my tobacco ration, a tin of ticklers, and I would swop that with the Irish bum-boats that came over from the Free State side. And if you were going out they would provide you with food and eggs stuff like, and I swapped my half pound of tobacco for a live hen and some eggs. I was under the impression that the hen would probably lay some more eggs, but it wasn't like that. And I was told by the leading hand of the mess that, whatever else I did, they were very happy to have the eggs, but I was to keep that damn chicken somewhere else. So I got a cardboard box and made a coop of a sort and secured it in the lee of the funnel. We didn't have any straw, so we tore up newspaper for its bedding, and I fed it on cornflakes and whatever, bits of bread, anything we could find.

A chicken at sea is quite interesting because its got a head and a body and they are joined by a fairly long neck, and when the ship rolls the body moves and the head stays still, and the neck which is joining them is nearly always in a sort of inverted position, so this chicken looks very odd when it's being subjected to the motion of a ship. Anyway, before I could keep that thing I had to apply to the commanding officer for permission to keep a pet. And so I duly applied through the coxswain and he said it had never been done before, 'but I suppose so, but why do you want to keep a chicken?', and I thought for fairly obvious reasons, as I thought we were going to get some more eggs. We never got another egg. And a fortnight out I remember very clearly sitting on the depth-charge rails, plucking this chicken, which we then cooked and there was this lovely chicken. Everybody else was on bullied beef and whatever it was. We had roast chicken, just myself and my mess, and I think we had to give a leg to the cook in the galley so he'd cook it properly. (*Arthur*)

We had cats principally. We did have a dog, two dogs, but cats were the main animal. Got on very well. Didn't seem to have any complaints by anyone that they shouldn't be there, you know; they accepted them. (*Dykes*)

We had a cat, 'U-boat' the cat. An incredible little animal – nobody taught it anything but it taught itself things. And I don't know where it came from. But one of the seamen made it a little hammock and a little life-jacket, and when action stations went that cat would make a beeline for the galley and he'd jump up on the flour bin, and he'd stay there until it was secure, and he'd jump down and go back up to the fo'c's'le again. When we got into harbour he'd go ashore. As soon as the ship was tied up alongside, he was ashore. And he would reappear,

HMS Snowflake, *Petty Officer George Mumford with the ship's dog, 1942* (courtesy Cyril Hatton)

with anything up to half an hour before we sailed. Don't ask me how he knew, but it was always the day that we sailed. Sometimes, as I say, within half an hour of sailing, he'd stroll down the jetty. And there was one occasion when he hadn't come back, and half the blokes were talking about jumping ship. They said, 'Well, this is it; this is our last trip. We're going to cop it this trip. U-boat's gone. He's not coming back.' And we'd actually cast off and the ship was gradually moving away from the dock, and I suppose there was probably a 6-foot gap, and this little grey bundle came hurtling down the dockside, took a flying leap and just about made it, clawed it's way on board, and then just sat there and washed itself. And we never knew, never knew how that cat knew when to come back.

He had a birthday on board. I mean he'd been on board about a year, I suppose, and somebody said, 'Oh, U-boat's birthday,' and, you know, the custom in those days of sippers was that, if somebody had a birthday, everybody in the mess gave them a sip of their tot, you see. So somebody said, 'Oh right, sippers all round for U-boat.' U-boat finished up with a good tot of rum. It was put in the saucer and put in front of him, and he just turned his nose up. So the chef put some evaporated milk in it – because we didn't have fresh milk; we only had tinned milk – stirred it up, and he drank the lot. The galley was right opposite the sick bay, and I was in the sick bay and I was watching, and you could see this cat getting drunk; you could see the rum having the effect. And his ears began to flap, until they were sort of parallel with the top of his head, and his eyes went all bleary. He looked at the deck and you could see him trying to judge the distance. He jumped off, and fell in a big heap. He just collapsed in a big lump. Then he got to his feet and he tottered to the hatch, and there was a combing in the hatch, about 9 inches high, and he put one leg at a time over the combing, flopped down the other side, crawled out through a coil of rope, climbed up, fell in, out, absolutely sparked out. And I thought, well, that's it, he's had it. It'll kill him. He's dead. Nothing I can do – couldn't go stomach pumping a cat. Anyway, left him alone, and I suppose about six o'clock in the afternoon a little head appeared over the coil of rope, ears flat back, and he looked terrible. He'd got the most awful headache, you could see. And he went out on the upper deck, was violently sick, came back in, went back in his coil of rope, and slept it off till the next morning, and he was right as rain. But you'd only got to give him a smell of rum after that and he was gone.

He finally left the ship under extraordinary circumstances. It's almost an unbelievable story, because he was so clean, he never fouled below deck; he always went on the upper deck. But on this occasion, for some reason, he did. And he couldn't have chosen a worse place: he picked the captain's chair, the captain's place in the wardroom. Of course, the captain saw it, 'What's all this about you see?', he said. 'Right, it goes in my report; put the cat in my report.' I

HMS Poppy's *ship's cat, 'Monty', eats his depth-charged caught fish in the Hebrides,* 1944 *(courtesy Ted Kirby)*

should tell you that the cat had been put on the official complement – last one on the complement – 'U-boat, ship's cat'. It turns up at defaulters with the chef carrying the cat, and the coxswain came down to me and he said, 'How do I put it; how do I put the charge doc?', he said. 'I can't say – on the captain's table. What do I say?' So I just said, 'Well, just say defecated.' So he said, 'Oh, alright.' So he went up to captain's defaulters. Captain stands at his little desk and coxswain calls out, 'Ship's cat, U-boat, off caps.' And the chef takes his cap off and he reads the charge out that U-boat did defecate at the captain's table (they're all mad, you know), and the captain said, 'Have you anything to say?' And, of course, chef had to speak for the cat saying, 'No sir, sorry sir, just caught short, sir.' And he said, 'Right! Punishment to be put ashore in Newfoundland and not to be admitted aboard.' And everybody was very wound up about this. They thought this is a bit much. But the extraordinary thing was, that cat went ashore of his own accord when we got to St John's and we never saw him again. He never ever came back. He just went. (*Goldsmith*)

CHAPTER SIX

THE BAD TIMES
AND THE GOOD

I enjoyed every minute of it. I mean, looking back, I suppose there was bad times. You forget. I mean, the things like hauling people out of the water and that sort of thing. You forget it. You remember the good times.

Raymond J. Donkin, RN, 1942–1946;
Leading Signalman, HMS WEAR

The corvetteers look back at their time in the corvettes during the Battle of the Atlantic with mixed feelings. Paradoxically, it was both a hellish and a happy time for them. What remains, it seems, is the memory of the tedium of the experience, the vicissitudes of the weather, the fear of getting killed and the worry they had for their families. They longed simply to be able to return home safely. On reflection, they appear to see a futility in it all. Yet such reflections are coupled with both a sense of pride and a sense of angst. They were proud of their own and their fellow seamen's achievements, but they envy the now lost strength and endurance they recall of their past selves. Furthermore, ironically they remember their time in corvettes as a happy time. They feel that they then benefited from a genuine sense of camaraderie – one they have never experienced since. The horrors of their ordeals, however, they prefer, understandably, never to experience again nor to have anyone else witness them. Indeed, many have not spoken of this dark, dark side of their history since the days it happened. The memories have remained vivid but locked within them for fifty years. Only the circumstances of the interviewing has allowed them to articulate that which is painfully difficult to articulate.

'The Fear Was a Sort of Cold Fear'
STRESS AND ANXIETIES

The fear was a sort of cold fear. That if you were in the
mess-deck and you heard this ping, and you realized . . .
you can hear the water passing the plates, if you're
on the lowermost deck, you can hear the water
rushing past the vessel, and you realize that there
was just, was it a ¼-inch, ⅛-inch, very thin bit of
steel between you and whatever.

ARTHUR

I was only frightened twice. Once was when we were frozen up, you know, when we were wallowing – that was frightening. The second occasion was when we were off Freetown, off to a convoy, and I was on the pom-pom gun lookout and I saw a white streak coming towards me and I thought, 'Crikey, a torpedo.' And I know for a fact that the hairs on the back of my neck stood up. But it was so quick that I never had time to contact the bridge and we heard this one almighty thump on the starboard side, and it was a barracuda fish – crikey. And I can honestly say that was the only time that I was ever frightened. No other way was

I ever frightened. I couldn't swim and I'd been dropped in the middle of the ocean in a boat, but somehow I had confidence in all those around me. I don't know why it was; it was an uncanny feeling. It seemed to me that the sea wasn't deep; it was always just a road to me. I don't know why. Good job it was, because if I'd thought, 'Crikey, that sea's about 3 miles deep and I can't swim!' (*Stephens*)

There was always that little fear, I think. Yes, but certainly when you were standing by your depth-charge you were not afraid, the adrenalin was running. I wouldn't call it fear. I don't know when fear came into it. (*Arthur*)

I think because we were constantly on the alert, constantly waiting, looking for things, then we came to accept this, what we now call stress. It was anxiety in those days. I suppose worry, too. Worry if you'd get back, because no doubt sometimes – again it depended on how the immediate emergency took you. One day you could get up on the upper deck and accept what you were going to do. But at night-time you could find that it unnerves you completely. You might be shaking possibly. It's the only time that I've ever smoked – to calm the nerves. We did a lot of smoking, as can be imagined, but I think that's basically why it was, because [at night] you couldn't see anything. You didn't know what was happening and, for heaven's sake, if you were hit there, in the darkness, there was little chance that you'd be picked up. Daytime yes, there was a good chance, but at night there was no chance, not for a corvette, because there weren't enough corvettes to start with on a convoy and they would be very occupied. They might come back for you at daylight, but between you finding yourself a survivor and that could be sufficient hours for you to lose your life. Yes, there was tension, but I cannot recall it affecting anyone to the extent that they needed medical treatment. (*Dykes*)

HMS Clematis, *Petty Officer Reynolds, 1942* (*courtesy Frank Richmond*)

Iris and Dick Dykes, Southend, June 1940 (*courtesy Dick Dykes*)

Of course, I was young – early twenties. Although the danger was always there, as soon as you left harbour there was always the danger, I think this also gave us some sense of excitement, too. It kept the adrenalin going, I think, that's the best way of putting it. (*Richmond*)

I think there was a large degree of anxiety with it. Particularly when you would leave harbour and you know very well within about an hour you could be having a good scrap. You wouldn't know when you might be hit or attacked. If you were attacked then it would be very sudden and over very quickly, because the ships were small. There wasn't much in them so far as watertightness was concerned, and so a torpedo that might hit the engine room or the boiler room – you'd just go down. I think there was one particular instance where a rating who was in the crow's nest of one of the corvettes that was torpedoed, he just really didn't get time to get out of the crow's nest. As the ship rolled over he was washed out. It was as quick as that. But I think you also got a fatalistic approach to it. That, well, if it hits us, well, possibly we might remember it; possibly we won't. There's not much else you could do.

It was always nice to get back to harbour and you always looked forward to it. When you first saw the seagulls, some 100 or so miles off Ireland, you knew you weren't very far from the United Kingdom. It was a pleasant sight to see the seagulls and even smell the Irish coast, you know. It has a smell about it. Peat, I suppose. It made you realize you weren't far from home. (*Dykes*)

I wouldn't call it stress. But what had happened, the captain had ordered the survivor nets over the side, because we thought we were going to pick up German survivors, and we would have done had it not been for picking up another asdic contact. And one of the chaps on board had lost a brother to the Germans. He was very, very bitter about it, and as fast as they put the nets over he was going along with his sheath knife and cutting through the ropes, so that if they had got on the nets, the nets would have broken and they would have gone back in the drink again. But that was the only incidence I ever saw. I wouldn't call that stress. It was probably more revenge than anything. (*Goldsmith*)

Later on, when I was under fire from a friendly merchantman and seeing the Oerlikon shells come across, I found that a little bit frightening, but only afterwards. When you see the Oerlikon shells with the tracers coming towards you and you hear a few bangs around, you think, this is a bit scary. It's rather like driving a car, I suppose, when you have a near miss on the motorway, or whatever it is, it affects you afterwards and not at the time. I think that's right. [You go into a bit of shock.]

When I served in *Duckworth*, which is a frigate and where I was sub-lieutenant, my action stations was on the forward gun, the gun layer was hit by this friendly American [ship], and when somebody is actually hit and you're next to him, and you see the stuff coming over. . . . But you're disciplined in the sense that you know what to do if this sort of thing happens. This is what naval discipline's about. It's not a question of standing up and saluting but, in this situation, you do it by numbers, it comes to you automatically. I think that's probably what discipline's all about in the armed services. It's not parade-ground stuff, it's survival, because you know what to do next. (*Arthur*)

He might mention one or two things. But very often he looked so ill and gaunt that one didn't have to ask what he'd gone through or what they had all been through.

It took him years really to settle down. Quite a few years after he was demobbed. Obviously he was having nightmares. He used to yell out, 'Abandon ship' and things like that. It really was devastating for them. (*Iris Dykes*)

'I Would Say Hellish; It Really Was'

REFLECTIONS

I would say hellish; it really was. You lived from day to
day wondering what was happening. I wouldn't want to
go through it again. I wouldn't want to see anybody
have to go through that again.

IRIS DYKES

It's only recently that he has spoken about a few things that he had encountered, sad things, you know. But never before. I don't think you like talking about it, do you? It's that sort of horror that they want to shut out. There must have been a lot.

It was a long time ago, but still it's there isn't it, in your mind. You can't forget it. (*Edith Hollinshed*)

Vivid memories I suppose were visual ones of the fine weather. And when it was beautiful, it was superb, with the Gulf Stream, with absolute clarity of vision, no industrial haze, nothing. There was that. There was the excitement of a landfall, always the excitement of a landfall. The smell of the land, coming in at night. But most of the time it was fairly boring because there was no excitement. There was the excitement occasionally when the submarines were about, that was true, but most of the time you had to be always alert. You always had to keep a good look out and you weren't told to, you just did. You would look forward to your meals, you would look forward to your hammock and you lived really from watch to watch. (*Arthur*)

And, of course, being the age that I was, you know, I never thought about these things. In actual fact, as I read books now I think to myself, 'If I knew that when I was there I'd be worried to death. I'd be sitting on the upper deck with a lifebelt on.' And talking about that, we did have a chap, a three-badge able seaman, now he was about thirty-two. 'Course, they were old men to us, once you'd got three badges at the age of thirty, it was one foot in the grave sort of thing. And he, when we were at sea, would never go below decks. He spent all his life on the upper deck, behind the funnel. And we used to take food up to him. When he was so scared, he wouldn't come down below decks until we got very close to the harbour. He was what they call the 'Tanky'. He assisted the supply chap in the cutting up of meat and that sort of thing, and issuing out the provisions that we'd got. (*Grant*)

The terrible thing of being shaken for your watch at four o'clock on a filthy morning, when you got out of a warm hammock to go on the upper deck, and you'd find that the wind and the snow, sleet, whatever, would be biting and you'd have to be four hours there. You'd change position from the wing of the bridge to the pom-pom position or whatever every hour. You'd have cocoa brought round, Kye – a naval traditional Kye. Pretty filthy stuff, but we all loved it. It was made of solid bars of chocolate scraped in the thing with hot water. It kept us going through the night. I'm sure it was very good for you. It was that awful business of having to get out of your hammock onto the deck, and then survive those four hours, without much exercise, no jumping about, you'd have to keep as warm as you could. And then you went and if you had that morning watch between four and eight you went down and you had your breakfast and you knew that you'd be falling in for another three or four hours' work, probably chipping paint. But the warmth of the company, the people of your own mess – there was that family feeling all the time. And people looked after you; you looked after them. I've never experienced it ever again quite the same. Wardroom is different. Wardroom, yes, there is a family feeling; it's not the same as that sort of warmth and that comfort of shipmates that you get on the lower deck in the small ship. (*Arthur*)

It is the futility of the whole aspect of war at sea. You're escorting forty, possibly fifty, ships and they're carrying cargoes of all manner of complexion. Items that have been made by someone, items that have been grown by someone over many, many months in the past and the ship is sunk, and it all goes to the bottom and it all seems to be such a terrible waste of time, of effort to me. It's not only the corvette people; it's the people in the factories that made the ships, that made the equipment, made the munitions that we used. There's so many hundreds of civilians involved in it as well as ourselves.

There's nothing more sorrowful or harrowing really than to see a ship sink and to hear it sink. There are noises that come from that ship as if, you might say, it's screaming as it sinks. Most of that noise that you hear is the cargo inside: the boilers, the engine, all moving from one end of the ship to the other. You see the aircraft and the tanks and the lorries which are on the upper deck sliding off into the sea, amongst the survivors, as it sinks, as it turns over. So all this equipment is thrown into the sea amongst the men. It seems to be so pointless that, as I said, people have patiently grown wheat, for a very long time, in Canada or America, only for it to be lost at sea, by some man firing a torpedo into the ship. Or the loss of life because of it. Because there have been some terrible deaths, you know. In my imagination I can see what it must be like inside the ship, the boiler room or engine room of a ship

DSC and medals of Lieutenant Roy 'Dick' Dykes, DSC, VRD (*Royal Naval Museum Collection*)

that's torpedoed, because as they go down the engines are still moving, and you get [everything sliding], the engines working inside the ship and the crew inside the ship in the engine room. They wouldn't stand a chance whatsoever in any way. (*Dykes*)

In the passing of the years, they've merged one into the other and one can only remember the tedious running backwards and forwards across the Atlantic. And the weather, particularly the gales, the movement of the boat, the exhaustion of working four hours on and four hours off, without getting a continuous night's sleep, and the relief of, when eventually hitting port, to be able to go to sleep and recuperate. (*Richmond*)

We saw this little ship, like a cork on the ocean, and when you see the terrific seas it used to contend with and then right itself and come out of all that, and you think, 'Well, if she can do it, we can do it.' And it was like a love between the crew and the ship, and that went all through the ship's company, right down from the skipper, right down to the lowest OD [Ordinary Seaman]. It was a love of the ship. It's like if you had a lovely home, you make it your home. Because it was our home for three years. When you leave it, you cry. And when those ships were paid off – after the war they were run up on the mud flats – grown sailors cried and I quite believed them because there was that love between them. You thought, 'Well, this ship's looked after me through three years of heavy seas, calm seas, rough seas, snow, the lot. And we've come through together.' And to suddenly think you're finished. It was as though the bottom had fallen out of your life. That's how I would describe it. And today when we have our reunion, it's all as though we're back together on one big ship, one big corvette, and there's that lovely feeling of comradeship again. This is what corvette life's about. You mightn't get it on a big ship. You might. I'd never know, because I've never been on a big ship, but I know full well that members who've been on big ships and been on corvettes say, 'The happiest time of my sea life was when I was aboard a corvette.' (*Stephens*)

THE FLOWER CLASS CORVETTE ASSOCIATION

'Without haste, but unresting.'

(FCCA motto)

The sense of camaraderie of which the men of the 'Flower' class corvettes all speak has been emulated to a certain extent through the fellowship of an association they formed. Such an association cannot, of course, re-create the exact comradeship they once felt. Through their association, though, the veterans can relate, knowing they have shared experiences and assumptions in life which they need not necessarily talk openly about but which they know the other has some real understanding of and empathy with. They can also, through their association, keep alive the memory of those experiences and the comrades they have lost both during the war and in the peace since. And for many, it seems, this is an important means for them to validate and authenticate their own experiences.

The association was formed in May 1981, when thirty-six ex-members of the 'Flower' class corvettes met at the Leamington Spa Royal Naval Association Club. Today the association has a worldwide membership of 1,180 full and 100 associate members. A reunion is held each year in Leamington Spa, followed by a church service and parade. Also, a Sea Sunday Service is held on the first Sunday in September in the village church of All Hallows at South Cerney in Gloucestershire.

The association has its own standard, a gift from Mr Denis Abbott, ex-HMS *Verbena*. It also has a beautifully engraved glass bowl presented to the association by Kenneth Hannan (USN *Tenacity*), ex-HMS *Candytuft*. [In addition] a model of HMS *Picotee* was commissioned by the association and made by Michael Cox. The association now has its own march ('The Corveteer'), composed by musician Dennison, Royal Marines School of Music.

Full membership is open to all those who served in 'Flower' class corvettes. Associate membership to relatives of full members. (*Stephens, from a letter*)

The crest of the Flower Class Corvette Association (Royal Naval Museum Collection)

I founded the association. I started off in 1980, when I wanted to try and contact some of my *Orchis* boys,

*Ronald James in his Flower Class Corvette Association blazer with badge and tie,
Southampton, 1994 (Royal Naval Museum Collection)*

so I put a piece in the *Navy News* asking anyone from the *Orchis* to get in touch with me, and had a fellow write to me who was a leading seaman when we first commissioned. I knew him because of his name, Larry Denzell, and there was a boxer by that name. I said, 'I know you. I can recall you.' I then said, 'The fellow I recall most is Mansell. Where's Mansell?' And he said he was working in Devonport Dockyard. And so I wrote to the personnel officer of Devonport Dockyard and within ten days had Mansell on the books. Meanwhile, Bob Davis from Malden wrote to me and said, 'Wouldn't it be a good idea if you wrote to the *Navy News* again and asked all corvetteers to get in touch,' so I did just that. I also wrote to two hundred newspapers to publicize the fact we were starting this association. Well, Bob came down to see me, the back end of 1980, or it would be early 1981, and we had a little chat and he said, 'Well, let's see if we can get a little bit of a reunion going.' He said on the way back to Malden – he came from Malden – he said, 'I'll call in at the two or three naval associations, see if they can accommodate us.' He called at Birmingham; they didn't want to know. Then he called in at Leamington Spa and they welcomed us with open arms. And so, ever since then, we've made Leamington Spa our base.

[Is this what's called Stevo's Navy?] Stevo's Navy? This is, well, it's only a joke. Because I get letters sent to me, 'Admiral' and all this nonsense, and it's only the camaraderie of the corvettes coming out again, you see. 'Stevo' is because of the nickname for Stephens, which you carried during the ship. You were always called 'Stevo', or 'Chalky White', or 'Dusty Miller', and I was called 'Stevo'. And I'd always get known by that.

We had a Christmas card printed once, and whether that was the motto that was allocated to the *Orchis* – 'without haste, but unresting' – [I don't know], but I thought, when we started this association, it typified a corvette, because it wasn't in a hurry, it wasn't fast and it was never still. So I thought, 'without haste, but unresting'. I thought that typical, and we adopted that as our motto for the 'Flower' class corvettes. (*Stephens*)

SELECT BIBLIOGRAPHY

Barnett, Correlli. *Engage the Enemy More Closely: The Royal Navy in the Second World War*, London, Hodder & Stoughton, 1991.

Behrens, C.B.A. *Merchant Shipping and the Demands of War*, London, HMSO and Longmans Green and Co., 1955.

Boutilier, James A. *RCN in Retrospect, 1910–1968*, Vancouver, University of British Columbia Press, 1982.

Brown, D.K. 'Atlantic Escorts, 1939–1945', International Historical Conference to Commemorate the Battle of the Atlantic, 1939–1945, Merseyside Maritime Museum, 26–28 May 1993.

Chalmers, Rear-Admiral W.S. *Max Horton and the Western Approaches: A Biography of Admiral Sir Max Kennedy Horton*, London, Hodder and Stoughton, 1954.

Creighton, Rear-Admiral Sir Kenelm. *Convoy Commodore*, London, William Kimber and Co., 1956.

Evans, George Ewart. *The Days that We have Seen*, London, Faber & Faber, 1975.

Gretton, Vice-Admiral Sir Peter. *Convoy Escort Commander*, London, Cassell, 1974.

———. *Crisis Convoy: The Story of HX231*, London, Peter Davies, 1974.

Howarth, Stephen and Law, Derek, (eds). *The Battle of the Atlantic, 1939–1945: The Fiftieth Anniversary International Naval Conference*, London, Greenhill Books, 1994.

Jones, Geoffrey. *Defeat of the Wolf Packs*, London, William Kimber and Co., 1986.

Lamb, James B. *The Corvette Navy: True Stories from Canada's Atlantic War*, Toronto, Macmillan, n.d.

Lynch, Thomas G. *Canada's Flowers: History of the Corvettes of Canada, 1939–1945*, Halifax, Nova Scotia, Nimbus Publishing, 1981.

Mason, Jr, John T. *The Atlantic War Remembered: An Oral History Collection*, Annapolis, Maryland, United States Naval Institute, 1990.

Monsarrat, Nicholas. *The Cruel Sea*, London, Cassell, 1952.

Poolman, Kenneth. *Focke-Wulf Condor: Scourge of the Atlantic*, London, Macdonald and Janes, 1978.

Preston, Antony and Raven, Alan. *Man O'War 7: Flower Class Corvettes*, London, Arms and Armour Press, 1973.

Rohwer, Jurgen. *The Critical Convoy Battles of March 1943*, London, Ian Allan, 1977.

—— *Axis Submarine Successes, 1939–1945*, Annapolis, Maryland, United States Naval Institute, 1983.

—— and Hummelchen, G. *Chronology of War at Sea, 1939–1945*, London, Greenhill Books, 1972, reprinted 1992.

Schull, Joseph. *Far Distant Ships: An Official Account of Canadian Naval Operations in World War II*, Toronto, Stoddart, 1950.

Scott, Morin. *War is a Funny Business*, Bognor Regis, Square Rigged Services, 1989.

Shean, Max. *Corvette and Submarine*, Claremont, Western Australia, Max Shean, 1992.

Thomas, David A. *The Atlantic Star, 1939–1945*, London, W.H. Allen, 1990.

Van Der Vat, Dan. *The Atlantic Campaign: The Great Struggle at Sea, 1939–1945*, London, Hodder & Stoughton, 1988.

Young, John M. *Britain's Sea War: A Diary of Ship Losses, 1939–1945*, Wellingborough, Patrick Stephens Ltd, 1989.

INDEX

Illustration references are in *italics*

A-brackets *38*
Abbott, Denis 148
accidents to ships 69
accommodation 90–98
acoustic torpedoes 53
Adams, Lieutenant 7
aircraft
    cover for convoys 37–8, 43
    Liberator shot down *35*, 86
    enemy 32, 47, 63
Ambler, George *110*
Argentia (Newfoundland) 36, 49, 119–20
Arthur, John xiii
asdic (submarine detection device) 43, 64, 65, 67
Atkinson, Sir Robert, DSC xiii

Baker, Officer 'Bagsy' 19–20
Barnett, Correlli: *Engage the Enemy More Closely* xxiii–xxiv
Bath (ship) 70
baths 108
Battle of the Atlantic viii, xxiii–xxiv, xxvii, 31, 32
beer 106
Brown, D.K: *Atlantic Escorts 1939–1945* ix
bunks 94–5
    see also hammocks
burial at sea 81, 83, 86

Canadian Star survivors *73*, *82*, *83*, *84*
Canham, Donald F. xiii, *95*, *117*
    extract from diary 78
Canham, Helen xiv
caning 8
card playing 115, 116
cargoes of merchant ships 39, 143
Carley float racing *115*

Castle class corvettes 2, 53
cats on board 133–6, *136*
censorship 125
Chatham Royal Naval Barracks 11
Chesterman, Harold G. xiv
chicken on board 133
Chief Petty Officers' 'perks' 11, 106
cigarettes *see* smoking
clothing 109–12
    FCCA uniform *149*
    RN uniform 17, 111, 116, 128
    overalls 17, 70, 110
    survivor kits 82, 83, 85
    wet weather gear 110, 111–12
Clyde 36
coal galleys 101
codes 24–5, 125
    Enigma 54–5
compass 2, 45
comradeship 18–21, 138, 143, 144–5
convoys 30–41
    length of journeys 98
    number of ships 24, 37, 41
    speed 37, 38, 40
    stragglers 34, 40, 58, 61, 86
    tail-end Charlies 36, 39
    HX229: 71
    HX231: 41
    ONS5: 32–3, 55
Coombs, Lieutenant 7
Cox, Michael 148
Cox, Tom 16, 129–30
crew, structure of 14–21
    captains 16, 18
    coxwains 14, 16, 17
    engine room personnel 14, 16, 27–8
    lieutenants 14, 16
    petty officers 23, 28, 106
    quartermasters 26
    seamen, able/ordinary 26

Escort Zone
Newfoundland Escort Force

THE N

Approximate limit of air cover from July 1941

Quebec

St John
Argentia

Sydney

Halifax

New York

Convoys disperse onward to
Quebec, New York, Kingston a
the South Atlantic

THE NORTH A

CONVOY ROUTES
THE 'FLOWER' CLAS

Kingston